FRAN:

From Whitby to the Wild Yorkshire Moors

A true story of Edwardian romance and tragedy

JOY SMITH

2QT (Publishing) Ltd

First Edition published 2022 by
2QT Limited (Publishing)
Settle, N. Yorkshire

Publisher Disclaimer:
The events in this memoir are described according to the
author's recollection; recognition and understanding of the
events and individuals mentioned and are in no way intended
to mislead or offend. As such the Publisher does not hold any
responsibility for any inaccuracies or opinions expressed
by the author. Every effort has been made to acknowledge
and gain any permission from organisations and persons
mentioned in this book. Any enquiries should be directed to
the author.

Internal photographs supplied by the author.
Cover image: Watercolour by Joy Smith.
Printed by TJ Books Ltd, Cornwall.

A CIP catalogue record for this book is available
from the British Library.
ISBN 978-1-914083-51-8

ONE

AN UNEASY SILENCE descended around the breakfast table. The family gazed apprehensively as John Booth looked at the letter; as head of the household, it was his job to deal with it and usually letters only arrived in cases of extreme emergency. He examined the magnificent penmanship of the copper-plate writing on the envelope, then carefully extracted the letter and studiously examined it. Looking up, he paused for a moment while the family sat with bated breath and then solemnly announced, 'The letter is for Fran. It says, "Miss Fannie Elizabeth Booth, 14, St Ann's Staith, Whitby".'

Fran looked stunned. 'It's for me!' she stuttered. 'Oh, Father. What does it say?'

'Give your father a chance, dear,' Sarah reprimanded her. 'He needs time to think.'

John finished reading the letter, then made his decision. 'I think we should all hear what this letter says.' He checked that everyone was listening and frowned at Lily, who was finding it difficult to maintain her silence. 'Being ten years old does not mean you can fidget, Lily,' he reprimanded her. She squirmed.

He began to read. '"The Whitby School Inspectorate, having regard to her recent performance as a student teacher in their area, is pleased to offer Miss Booth the position of sole teacher at Howdale School, Fylingdales. The post will become available in the autumn term, 1899. We look forward to an early response".'

He looked at his daughter. 'My word, Fran. They must think a lot of you in the Whitby schools. What do you think about that?'

Fran flushed with excitement and embarrassment. 'Oh, Father! I'm thrilled. What a lovely surprise. I had no idea this was coming.' Then her face changed and she looked unsure and apprehensive. 'You will let me accept their offer, won't you?' she pleaded.

Sarah intervened. 'Your father and I will have to consider this carefully, Fran dear. A decision like this can't be made without thought for its implications. We'll let you know in due course. I suggest we all go about our work today and give Father time to think.'

She turned to Mary. 'I think I heard the lodger call, dear. You should go and see what he wants. And you, Lily, must get off to school ... and don't forget you have a pianoforte lesson this evening. You must be home on time.'

The breakfast gathering broke up.

Left alone, Sarah prepared for a day of baking as she wrestled with her dilemma. On the whole, she was proud of her daughters. Hannah was caring for an elderly couple who spoke highly of her, Mary was a godsend who looked after the lodgers and Lily, despite her youth, was obviously a talented pianist and took after her father with her needlework, for John was a fine tailor. Of course, Rose was always causing problems because she seemed to think it was her mission in life to help the needy. She worked for the Poor Law Authority and seemed to like the job but, in Sarah's opinion, got far too involved with her clients. She even seemed happy in her squalid, rented accommodation in Easterby's Yard.

'Ridiculous!' Sarah muttered to herself. 'Rose will be the death of me. But Fran – I never thought she would cause me worry. It's her ridiculous imagination that's the problem. Why on earth can't she be content with what she's got?'

Yet Sarah knew it was a tremendous compliment to the girl that the school board had offered her a job. It was an even bigger compliment that they thought she could take on the responsibility of running a school single-handedly at only nineteen years old. But Howdale School was remote. It catered for the children of farming families who wrenched a living from the moorland that surrounded it, families that had a reputation for being wild and ill-mannered.

'Oh, dear,' she mused. 'To think that I am from Pearson stock! My grandfather would turn in his grave if he thought that one of his family would consider working out on the moors. That lovely jet bust of a Negro that he made for the 1861 Paris Exhibition was the product of a family whose women do not work amongst heathens!'

Sarah had made up her mind; she would make sure that Fran did not accept the job.

Mary joined her in the kitchen. 'What do you think to that?' she asked. 'Fancy Fran being offered a job at Howdale! She's so excited, Mother. They must think very highly of her.'

'Or perhaps no-one else wants the job!' Sarah retorted. 'Whoever is stupid enough to accept a job like that will have to lodge somewhere nearby, for it's far too remote to travel to every day. And in winter they'll be cut off by terrible snowdrifts. No, dear, I don't think that job is for Fran!'

Mary looked uncertain. 'She'll be so disappointed, Mother. You know how much she loves teaching, and this could be her chance to prove her worth. She's young and she's healthy. It would be such an adventure, a chance to experience something different – to really live. Be honest, Mother, life here can be very staid for a young person with drive and ambition. Surely you and Father won't stop her from accepting such an offer!'

Mary was obviously intent on speaking up for her sister. As she left the room, she continued passionately, 'It must be so gratifying for her to know how much her work is valued. I wish I was lucky enough to have that sort of praise.'

Sarah was taken aback at Mary's tirade, and her expression changed to one of concern. 'But your work is valued, Mary! You know how much the family appreciates all that you do, and we're not hard taskmasters! Why, you know my attitude to housework – I've encouraged you girls to litter our home! Your proliferation of bits and pieces meant that you used your imaginations to paint, to draw, to knit, to sew, to read, to appreciate music – in other words, to put your time on this earth to good use. I've never allowed you to be bored, for a person who claims to be bored is generally a boring person. And I drilled you in the skills of etiquette, in polite conversation, handling your cutlery correctly, using the right forms of address to those you meet. Really, dear, I don't think you have much to complain about.'

Mary smiled and, in a more forgiving tone, tried to pacify her mother. 'I wasn't complaining, Mother. I was just slightly envious of Fran. And I was thinking that the encouragement you've given us to use whatever talents we have has paid off for her. I didn't mean to cause offence.'

As Mary left, Sarah paused in her baking. The flour she had sifted into a bowl stood unused on the kitchen table as her mind raced and she reflected on the events that had led to this moment.

As soon as Fran had reached school-leaving age at thirteen, it was Sarah who had encouraged her daughter to work at Aunt Polly's school. At the time, the decision had seemed a good one. When she was seventeen, the local schools' inspectorate had approached Fran with the suggestion that she should become a fully-fledged teacher instead of simply assisting her aunt. Fran had duly become a student teacher.

But it had never crossed Sarah's mind that this would lead to an offer of a job on the moors. 'What on earth would the girl want to do that for?' she muttered. As she dusted the kitchen table with flour and began rolling out pastry, she questioned Fran's motives for leaving Whitby.

Sarah loved her home town and revelled in its vibrancy. She loved the market, where tinkers and pedlars tempted passers-by with their raucous shouts and tuneless but catchy refrains, and farmers came from the surrounding countryside to sell their dairy produce, vegetables, eggs and fruit. She delighted in the shops, many of them on St Ann's Staith, where there was a bookseller, a milliner, a photographic studio, a butcher, a cobbler and sweet shops. She enjoyed the busy harbour front where the litter of fishing tackle, boxes of fish being offloaded and fish sellers plying their wares clashed with the sights and sounds of coal merchants dragging their loads on carts and barrows through the narrow streets off the harbour.

She treasured the smells, the sounds, and the constant hubbub. She prided herself on being a denizen of a place where the newly arrived railway brought visitors to take advantage of the fresh air and to admire the fascinating geography and geology of the area. To her, living in Whitby was a privilege and to have one of her daughters apparently reject this privilege was anathema to her.

Only recently the family had moved from their tiny cottage in Church Lane to St Ann's Staith as a step closer to achieving Sarah's ambition to live in Flowergate. Now they had four bedrooms, which provided ample space for John and herself, their three daughters who still lived at home, and a lodger.

'Who in their right mind would leave such luxury and such promise for the future?' she said out loud. 'Who would exchange this for the moors?'

But Sarah had not convinced herself. She knew that Fran was energetic and physically strong, and that she loved social interaction of any sort, but particularly enjoyed the company of children. As she popped pies and pastries into the oven, she wondered whether the rigours of life on Howdale moor would be a challenge to which her daughter could and should rise.

Perhaps the routine of life at the Booth family home was not sufficient an outlet for a young lady with spirit and a sense of adventure. And the extra income would not come amiss. A new piano for Lily might be a possibility if Fran earned as much as she seemed to think she would.

She considered Mary's words. Mary was unequivocally in favour of her sister accepting the job. She had pointed out that life at St Ann's Staith was more restrictive than was always good for a girl with a lively sense of purpose. The comforting hubbub of noise and vibrancy of life outside her doorstep made Sarah feel part of Whitby life, but it reinforced her disquiet at the prospects of Fran going off to the lonely isolation of the moors. Yet she wondered whether she was assuming that her and her daughter's ambitions were one and the same.

She wondered whether she was guilty of selfishness in wanting her daughter to stay close by and live a life bound up in her own. She wondered if her fear of the moorland people was as well-founded as she had thought it was. In a whirl of uncertainty and confusion, she also admitted to herself that she did not want to cause bitterness and resentment in her daughter.

Fran came home that evening and was greeted by an agitated Sarah. 'Have you decided, Mother?' she asked.

Sarah was quick to respond. 'You know, dear, it is your father's job to make decisions.'

'Nonsense!' Fran surprised her mother. 'He's led by you – and you know it!'

'But the law is quite clear, dear. It is the men of this world who make decisions. Don't tell me you've started to think like your sister! Why, Rose reckons that women should have the vote. You know she's wrong. Men get us into the messes we face and it is men who should get us out of them.'

'But I'm not talking about world affairs, Mother, I'm talking about my life and my future. Do you not think that I am entitled to have a say in that, even if I am a woman? And–' Fran looked sheepish '–I don't like to remind you, Mother, but do you remember when you encouraged father to give up tailoring and try his hand in the jet industry? He hated it and he didn't make any money. You said you would never interfere with the family's natural inclinations and ambitions again!'

Sarah was taken aback. She was a Pearson; Pearson men made money and Pearson women made decisions about the household. She knew she had got carried away when she had assumed that John would have a similar talent to her forebears who worked with jet, but she'd been wrong. He simply didn't have the drive and ambition that the industry demanded. Was she now making a similar mistake in trying to influence her daughter's future? Just because John was a gentle, pliable individual, was she using the power that gave her in the wrong way?

She made up her mind: she would not stand in Fran's way. The girl would accept the offer of a new teaching post. Perhaps it was God's will that she should face a life that would be difficult but probably rewarding and, like a missionary, she might bring education and knowledge of His word to Fylingdales. The school was a Church of England foundation and, whilst, to Nonconformists like herself that was far from perfect, Fran would have the support of that church in her work.

'Leave it with me,' she told Fran.

When John arrived home for his dinner that evening, Sarah told him of her thoughts. He, of course, agreed, and when Fran sat down to eat, she was told she had her parents' blessing. She was thrilled. It was 1899, and it was nearly summer. Within a year, she would welcome in a new century, become independent, face adversity, but would doubtless overcome it. She would get to know new people and places. She was full of optimism and she was happy; she felt she had achieved success, and she felt thoroughly grown up. This was the beginning of a new life.

7

Two

In the middle of August, with her senses heightened by nervous anticipation, Fran set out alone for a visit to Howdale school. As she looked out of the window of the train, the familiar waters of the River Esk flowing beneath the high viaduct seemed more dramatic than they had ever done when she'd used the route to visit Scarborough with her sisters. Away from the town, fragile arable crops, grazing sheep and breathtaking views across the cliffs and sea all combined to give a new perspective.

At Fyling Hall station she was met by a Mr Petty. He introduced himself and said that her predecessor had lodged with him and his wife in their cottage and he'd been asked to take her to the school. She sat beside him on his farm cart as they climbed a rough, steep track. Scrubland turned to moor and, as far as the eye could see, swathes of purple heather in full bloom took her breath away.

The magnificence of the scene and the silence, broken only by the sound of gulls in the distance, was to her imaginative mind justification for her decision to work there. The apprehension which she'd experienced was replaced with delight. And there, amid such glory, she saw a single-storey stone construction that nestled so firmly amongst the rocks and barren earth that it appeared to be part of the landscape: Howdale School.

Two people greeted Fran at the school, the inspector and her predecessor. The latter was a solidly built woman with white hair tied in a bun who said she had been at the school since the 1870s and offered any help she could give. Her detailed knowledge of both the area and the children in her care was outstanding and when she finally handed over the keys to the building, Fran began to have real doubts about her ability. But she had agreed to do the job.

Having had a guided tour of the stove, the lighting and care of which appeared to be at least as complicated as anything to do with teaching, she looked round the room with its flagstone floor, beamed ceilings and windows set deep in the solid stone walls and decided that perhaps this was the sort of challenge she needed.

The rest of the summer saw Fran preparing for the new term. She studied the register. There were twenty-nine children on the roll and she noticed a preponderance of names from the same families – nine were Pickerings, eight were Thompsons and the rest were Collinsons, Harlands, Stubbs and a few less well-represented names.

One of her mother's arguments against Fran accepting the job had been that it would throw her into a society where intermarriage was the norm and she would always be an outsider. Looking at the class register, she could see the basis on which Sarah's opinion had been formed. Hearsay in Whitby would have one believe that independence was viewed in high regard on the moors, and that townsfolk were generally despised as being too dependent on others and lacking an understanding of true hardship and deprivation. Fran feared she would fall short of the expectations of the local community, but there was no turning back. She had made her decision and now she had to live with it.

On the first day of term, Fran arrived early. Shortly afterwards, she was joined by a man in his early thirties with four children hovering uncertainly behind him. Clad in riding boots, heavy tweed trousers and jacket, and holding a tweed cap in his hands in deference to her presence, he introduced himself. 'I'm Gowan

9

Pickering, ma'am. Pleased t' meet thee. Welcome t' Howdale. Tha'll love this place. 'Tis as fine a part o' God's earth as tha'll ever see.'

'It is indeed magnificent,' Fran agreed.

Gowan Pickering looked pleased. 'Well, I should know! I were born and bred here, lass. My family farm most o' t' land tha' can see afore thee – from Thorney Brow to Low Flask Farm, Stoupe Brow, Haggard Hill, Brow Cottages ... even as far down as Farsyde House. But t' land's our life and thine's t' classroom! I'd like to talk to thee about my bairns.'

'You can approach me at any time to discuss your children, sir. How can I help?'

'T' farm's my life and I like it well,' he said. 'But it's a hard un. My lads'll see opportunities in t' twentieth century that I ne'er dreamed of, and I want 'em to tek full advantage. Wi' your help, and a good dose o' t' cane if necessary to mek 'em behave, these lads'll have t' chance to go far. Reginald's a bright lad if he puts 'is mind on it, and I'd like to see him go to t' grammar school in Whitby. T'others can be put ready to understand new ways o' doin' things. Their poor mother's health is na' good and she canna' help. I must leave 'em t' you.'

Fran assured him she would do her best with all her pupils and he smiled. He thanked her for her time and then introduced Reginald, aged nine, John Clark, aged eight, Ernest, aged six, and Gowan, aged five. He left just as the rest of the school arrived, all eager to see the new teacher and sometimes accompanied by parents or servants who introduced their charges and departed. The first day had begun.

Twenty-five inquisitive youngsters gazed at their new teacher with suspicion. She wished them good morning, told them her name and wrote it in clear letters on the blackboard, then opened the register to record their attendance. As soon as that task was complete, she told them to stand and begin the day with a hymn. She had chosen 'All Things Bright and Beautiful', and their voices joined hers in making a sound that seemed to spread across their surroundings, for the weather was warm and the school door stood open. The children sat, the morning's work began and, across the moors, a lone worker could hear the chanting of arithmetic tables.

◆ ◆ ◆

When Fran returned to Whitby at the end of her first half-term at Howdale, the family crowded round her to hear stories of her adventures.

'What's it like to be so far from home?' Mary wanted to know.

'Have you made the right decision, Fran? You must feel very lonely working single-handed,' a puzzled-looking Hannah queried.

'Is Mrs Petty feeding you properly?' her mother wanted to know.

'What a fantastic adventure!' from a wide-eyed Rose.

Fran tried to answer their questions, and her face lit up as she described her new life. It was obvious that she was happy. 'It's a lot like working at Aunt Polly's school,' she said. 'I suppose the children of Fylingdales are from very different backgrounds to the ones in Whitby, and they sound different when they speak, but at the end of the day they are children and you know I love working with children. And, yes, Mother, Alice Petty feeds me well. Why, her apple pies are nearly as good as yours!'

Sarah smiled, but she was obviously not convinced of her daughter's welfare. 'When you say the children are from different backgrounds, Fran, I suppose they're basically uncultured, wild moors' people. How on earth can you relate to them? I doubt any of them have so much as a piano in their homes!'

'Oh, Mother! You're so prejudiced! Young Reginald Pickering's a bright lad and confident. He even impressed the local vicar when I got him to recite the creed as proof that he was being well taught. I can't say I like the reverend, for he smells of garlic and seems to have an inbuilt dislike of children, but in a Church of England school I'm afraid I have to accept his periodic interference.' She smiled. 'And, although they may not all have pianos in their homes, I think if I needed practical assistance these children would be of more help than many of their town counterparts!'

'Oh, do tell,' said Mary. 'Tell us about some of them.'

'Well, there's a strong bond between most of them because they're inter-related,' Fran began.

'I told you!' her mother interjected. 'Intermarriage is known to be a trademark of moorland life.'

'But, Mother!' Fran countered. 'On the whole, these youngsters are sturdier than those from the poorer parts of Whitby. They have the benefit of fresh air and fresh food, and they revel in their close ties with nearby families. I'll give you an example. The Pickerings have nine children at the school already, and both Gowan Pickering and his brother, William, have toddlers at home. But Gowan's wife, Tamar, is a Thompson and she comes from a family of nine who married into the Collinson and Harland families, meaning that they all have cousins at the school.'

Sarah looked horrified. 'What a catalogue! I think I'll stick to my opinions, Fran. Those children will end up marrying their cousins and they'll see nothing of the outside world.'

'Mother! How much of the outside world do you see? You even thought my job at Howdale School was the equivalent of leaving for another world! They're children, they need schooling. And it's my job to teach them.'

Sarah looked annoyed. 'But I've got Whitby, not a barren moorland. I've got everything on my doorstep. Really, Fran, you can't compare.'

Fran ignored her mother's outburst. 'To go back to your question, Mary. Gowan Pickering's children are good examples of how individual each child can be. I've mentioned Reginald already. He's the eldest. John Clark is next, and he's very different. He's shy, easily reduced to tears, totally lacking in self-esteem. Thank goodness he's got his little cousin Edith, who likes him. She's only six years old, but she goes out across the moors with him and they collect grasses, ferns and such like for the nature table. Then there's Ernest, who simply wants to be with his father's pigs. Even his boots smell of pigs! He'll make a good pigman one day, but he's not good at schoolwork!' Fran chuckled. 'I think he only does what he has to for me because he thinks I might get out the cane!'

'Do you have a favourite?' asked Lily.

'Oh, Lily! You know I can't have a favourite.'

'Bet you do,' said Lily.

'Well, I have to admit that one of Gowan Pickering's children is everybody's favourite. He's called Gowan after his father – he's got such an infectious laugh and he's enthusiastic about everything! With his twinkling eyes and good looks, I can't help liking him. In fact, at lunchtime he nearly always seems to get an extra morsel of bread and dripping or a slice of fat off the boiled bacon from the other children. They all want to be Gowan's friend.'

'Well, I'm impressed that you've got to know your charges so quickly, dear, and I'm delighted that you're enjoying your work,' said Sarah. 'But I dread the winter. So far, you've only experienced Howdale Moor in good weather.

♦ ♦ ♦

As winter crept over Howdale, there were times when Fran wondered if her mother's forebodings were justified. Gale-force

13

winds howled across the bleak earth, rain lashed the rocks and waves crashed against the nearby cliffs. Her daily routine became increasingly uncomfortable and the schoolhouse more difficult to run. She had to arrive early enough to light the stove and, although she left it burning every evening, it did not stay alight and the room was chill and draughty the next day. Yet her imaginative mind revelled in the beauty that surrounded her: the wild moorland, farmland and rugged coast provided her with prospects that changed with the seasons and held constant pleasure. The school became her second home and she loved it.

At Christmas, Fran almost wished she was part of the moorland 'clans' when the children told her about noisy gatherings and tables laden with hams, chicken, pork, pies, cakes and trifles. She was returning to St. Ann's Staith where she knew her parents' Non-Conformism would mean celebrations that were far more formal. Yet she also recognised that life on the moors could be fragile. William Pickering and his wife, Mary, at Low Flask Farm had postponed their six-year-old daughter's admission to school because her health was poor. John Pickering at Haggard Hill had an eight-year-old daughter, but she also could not attend because of poor health. Gowan Pickering asked if she would accept his three-year-old daughter, Elizabeth Estill, because his wife's health was poor.

'Yes,' Fran had to admit when she talked to Rose about the deprivations she witnessed, 'the children of Howdale moor and the wider area of Fylingdales have a hard life.'

Rose was eager to point out that the people of Whitby, and especially the poorer classes, suffered in the same way. Whooping cough, measles, chickenpox and influenza were life threatening, but she had to admit that isolation meant that the moorland people often struggled alone.

◆ ◆ ◆

Having completed a full year at the school, a more confident and relaxed Fran took charge of the little schoolroom in the autumn term of 1900. The rigours of the winter that followed saw the end of an era with the death of Queen Victoria in January 1901.

In Whitby, the populace combined their feelings of sadness at the loss of their queen with an anticipation of burgeoning trade in jet, and reminders of the Queen and Empress could be seen in every shop, stall and home. In Fylingdales there was no such outpouring of grief. There was a service at St Stephen's Church, which was dutifully attended by the farming community, but generally the activities of the state, and its representative the Queen, had little relevance to their lives. In the schoolroom, Fran tried to inspire a sense of loyalty to Queen and country in her charges, but she was hard pressed to achieve more than token interest. More important to them was survival through the harsh winter and a longing to see the green shoots of spring push through the earth.

By the end of her second year at the school, Fran could reflect on the changes she had witnessed. She felt satisfied that she had played some part in widening the horizons of the children in her charge, but perhaps it was because she was in a reflective mood that the final term of the year made such a marked impression on her imaginative mind.

Her first realisation that something was wrong was when the Pickering children formed themselves into warring groups. The Thompsons allied themselves with Gowan's children, whilst their cousins, the children of Gowan's brothers, John and William, joined against them. Work was occasionally spoilt, clothes 'accidentally' torn, fights broke out amongst the boys and the girls became spiteful and restless.

A little research soon revealed the cause of the rift. Jane Pickering, grandmother to the Pickering children, had offered her home and farm to Gowan, her youngest son. His accommodation at Browside Cottage comprised only four rooms and Tamar, his wife, was pregnant with their eighth child. In the eyes of his two older brothers, this was simply another example of their youngest sibling being given preference over them. He was a powerful, hard working, charismatic individual, but in their eyes he was also spoilt. He was used to getting his own way but, on this occasion, he was being offered what they viewed as an unfair part of the family's inheritance. The anger and resentment that this feud caused was spilling over into the classroom.

For the first time since she had started the job, Fran felt that she was out of her depth. Dealing with a temperamental stove, coping in extreme weather conditions, comforting individuals in moments of pain or tragedy, encouraging achievement and nurturing talent were challenges she had risen to but the present dilemma seemed beyond her power to control. Not only was the atmosphere in the schoolroom toxic, but the worst personality traits of the children were revealed.

The end of the summer term saw a despondent Fran wave goodbye to her charges. She knew harvest time lay ahead and they would experience hard work. For some, there would be the misfortune of illness or damage to their young bodies as they struggled to cope with farm machinery or wayward livestock. But she also knew that the adults in this sad episode would become increasingly intransigent, and consequently the division of loyalties would be reinforced. It would take something fairly dramatic to restore the supportive climate she had worked so hard to foster and to re-forge friendships and loyalties that had been the trademarks of her schoolroom.

Her conjecture was accurate. The dramatic event that re-established Pickering loyalties came on Wednesday, the 14th of August 1901, during the summer holidays.

Fran was enjoying the summer, glad of the break. The weather was lovely, and she was standing on St Ann's Staith. Reminders of the morning's catch left by the fishermen permeated her senses. There was a smell of fish, the clutters of nets, chains and boxes, the boats rising and falling with the gentle waves, and the sound of ropes creaking as they fought to hold the boats steady. Nearby, an ice-cream vendor chatted to a gaggle of children eagerly reaching for his wares. Ladies with elegant, long dresses held parasols to ward off the damaging effects of the sun, and mothers gathered their children together, reprimanding those who had wet their clothes and shoes when they had succumbed to temptation and played in the water. Men stood in groups smoking and chatting, whilst others on horseback guided their mounts through the summer throng. Whitby, so different to Fylingdales, was its busy, noisy self.

A youth sidled up to her. She recognised him as one of the Harland boys who had left Howdale shortly after her arrival having had his thirteenth birthday. His face told her he had news for her.

'Have ye heard?' he asked.

She was puzzled.

'Mrs Pickering died this morning,' he announced.

Immediately, she assumed he meant Gowan's mother at Thorney Brow Farm.

'No, not 'er,' said the lad. 'I mean Mrs Pickering at Browside. She died having t' baby, Miss, and t' bairn's so sickly it's being baptised now. Dr Ross was there, Miss, but he couldna help.'

Fran felt numb and her head spun as she thought of the eight motherless children, including, if it survived, a fragile, newborn baby isolated on the moor; of old Mrs Pickering seeing eight of her grandchildren with an uncertain future; of the Thompson family losing a granddaughter, a daughter, and a sister. Her thanks to the boy who had brought the news were perfunctory.

She fled home, told her mother the news and wept. For her,

the summer sun had lost its splendour, and the noise and hub-bub of Whitby was blotted out of her mind. The day was no longer a holiday but a day of mourning.

The little school at Howdale was no stranger to tragedy, but the repercussions of this terrible event were likely to be felt across the wider community. At that moment in time, she could not imagine how the children of whom she had grown so fond would cope with the latest twist of fate that added yet another form of deprivation to that which they already knew.

THREE

JANE PICKERING HAD a reputation across Fylingdales as a lady to be reckoned with. Her husband, Gowan, had died in 1869 and, against the advice of all who had dealings with her, she had taken his place as head of the family. 'I'll not go into service and see my children looked after by others!' she had declared.

As a result, she had cared for her family, single-handedly run her home, Thorney Brow, and farmed its 270 acres. The isolated, stone-built house stood some 500 feet above sea level and looked out across magnificent moorland and a valley that swept down the cliffs and to the sea.

It had never been simply a family dwelling. The moorland in which it sat was better suited to pastoral than arable farming, so the welfare of livestock and the storage of both its means of sustenance and its products were as important as the welfare of humans. It provided shelter for both; it required self-sufficiency from those who lived within its walls, and it demanded dedication. It was the centre of a way of life and a business, and Jane loved it.

Tall, muscular, with a calmness in the face of adversity and robust good health, she had succeeded against the odds. Now her plans to retire had been thwarted and her pivotal role in the family's well-being was affirmed as Thorney Brow became home to three of her youngest son's children.

'Well, I'm getting past t' age to be mother to these youngsters,' she remarked over a cup of tea some days after her daughter-in-law's funeral. 'But there's nay choice! Between us, we'll cope.

We'll have to!'

'You took me in, Grandma, when my mother gave birth to Rebecca,' said Mary Ann. 'And, now it's my turn to help with Gowan's little ones.'

'Aye. And tha' mother's still a frail one, no doubt about it. But she's my son John's wife, and family must stick together. Why, t' Tyremans have done t' same. When Tamar died, her parents took in little Ernest while t'others at Thorpe had t' newborn. And t' Burdetts have made room for young Gowan up at Howdale Farm. Tha's a good lass, Mary. I've no regrets about taking thee in. Tha' pulls tha' weight around the house and farm, and tha' knows full well there's enough to do round here!'

Jane looked at Margaret. 'And I don't know how I'd manage wi'out thee, young Margaret! Tha's a good daughter and tha' might never ha' married, but tha's cared for enough children. Little Alfred's only eighteen months old, but he already loves his Aunty Margaret. And Ethel and Elizabeth will be off to school soon, but they need the care that all little 'uns need and tha's always so willing.'

Margaret smiled but made no response.

The little tea party broke up. The week after Tamar's funeral had been very little different to any other at Thorney Brow; livestock did not allow the luxury of a period of mourning. Never given to introspection, Jane took solace from the constant demands of farm life and revelled in the continuity it provided. There was no time for introspection, no time to grieve.

Like others of her generation, she had little time for outward displays of emotion. She had a stalwart acceptance of the inevitable and a deep respect for the dead, but her priority was with the living. The huge physical effort required at this time of year ensured that children were given the security that routine provided and adults could use exhaustion to mask their underlying emotions and sleep soundly. Gowan came every day from

Browside and, during the school holidays, his eldest boys, Reginald and John Clark, joined him. Now this meant feeding a family of nine. 'Thank God I've got Mary and Margaret to help,' she murmured.

But Jane was very aware of the fact that, although her daughter Margaret's life had been dominated by the need to help her mother, recently Margaret's mind had been elsewhere.

'Never!' she exclaimed. 'T' lass is thirty-seven years old. Surely no man'd want to tek her on when there's young lasses looking for a husband! If anyone in t' family needs to wed, it's poor Gowan. 'Tis too early after Tamar's death for him to think on it, but he's by himself now in that little cottage at Browside apart from 't lads, Reg and John. He's a man. He needs a wife.'

But Jane had not convinced herself. The more she thought about it, the more she realised Margaret had been preoccupied with a certain butcher from Robin Hood's Bay, Henry Newton. 'He was especially solicitous o' t' lass at Tamar's funeral,' she recollected.

There was no denying it, Margaret had a suitor. 'Perhaps t' lass deserves a bit o' personal happiness,' she thought. 'But how will I manage wi'out her? I think I need a word wi' young Henry.'

The next day, Jane harnessed the horse and cart and headed in the direction of the road to Bay Town, pausing only to acknowledge the greetings of her son, William, at Low Flask Farm. 'Thank God William and Mary manage so well,' she thought. 'Nine fine children and all o' them healthy.'

She skirted the village of Thorpe, now home to her newest granddaughter named Tamar after her mother. Gowan had brought his wife to Thorney Brow in the last stages of her labour and it was there that she had died. The Tyremans were Tamar's family and Gowan had saddled his horse and taken the swaddled baby to them on that terrible day.

Jane reflected on the hurried and rather unceremonious way

in which the young curate had ridden out to Thorney Brow and perfunctorily carried out his duties, blessing the wasted body of the mother and baptising the baby. Jane had an ambivalent attitude to the church. Her fear of the Almighty was genuine enough, but her understanding of God's representatives on earth was lacking, just as she always felt that their understanding of their flock was less than perfect.

'I suppose t' young lad did 'is best,' she concluded. 'T' Almighty'll tek Tamar, for t' lass did no harm and t' babe'll meet her maker as a baptised member of t' Church if she does'n' thrive. And I suppose I'm glad it were t' curate that did t' offices, for it's difficult to tek to t' vicar. He might be a learned man, but 'is ruddy complexion's got more to do with 'is liking for t' bottle than 'is love of t' land, and 'is forebears are monied folks wi' little in common wi' farmers like us.

'I might as well tek a detour and visit t' church yard while I'm about these parts,' she decided. Instead of heading straight to the Newton family's butchery as she had intended, she diverted her course along Church Lane to Old St Stephen's Church.

High on the eastern slopes of the hills that surround Robin Hood's Bay, this square, stone-built place of worship stood in isolation from other structures. Its solid, unprepossessing exterior, ornamented with nothing more than a basic bell tower and arched, unadorned windows, gave the visitor a feeling of timelessness and security. The view from its tiny, sheltered porch was magnificent. There were the hills and the ever-changing sea that, on this day, glinted in the sun; on another day it might roar and turn to deep grey. The moors stretched out spectacularly to Ravenscar, clad in their August cloak of purple heather.

The churchyard's tightly packed, disorganised and eclectic collection of headstones was, to Jane, a reminder of lives inextricably intertwined with her own, and her spirit was uplifted. 'I never could tek to t' new St Stephen's, for brick's no substitute for stone even wi' all t' fancy windows,' she had often remarked.

She made her way to the headstone that was most familiar, that of her husband, Gowan, their baby, Mary Ann, and their son, Thomas. She knelt by the side of the grave and cleared away the weeds that had partially obliterated the carved inscription.

It was now twelve years since Thomas's death, also at Thorney Brow, but she still puzzled as she always had at his lifestyle. He had left home to work as a butcher, first in Sleights and then in Scarborough. The railway had allowed her to see him occasionally, but he had not thrived in his new life. She had begged him to come back to the farm, but he seemed set on a life of his own. He had looked tired and pale, which she attributed to a lack of wholesome fresh air, and he had lost weight. She had decided it was because of a lack of home comforts; the Leake family, who owned the butchery where Thomas worked, provided accommodation but, in Jane's opinion, he needed a wife.

Jane took some solace from the fact that he had returned to Thorney Brow to die. She had known he was near his end when he had arrived on the train one chilly evening in late September 1889. He had struggled to walk to the farm, and she wished she had harnessed the cart to fetch him. Her own and Margaret's ministrations and prayers had done little to help. He had a cough, appeared to have a fever and, on a rainy, cold day in October, had passed away. Now he lay with his father and baby sister in the grave where she now knelt.

At least he was not alone. Not only was the grave adjacent to that of Jane's dead husband's brother, Matthew, but surrounding her were the graves of other women's children, some from her own family: her niece, Mary Ann, and nephew, John, who had died in the dreadful days of the 1860s. Mary Ann had been sixteen months old and John only five months. And there were babies within a matter of yards: little George Atkinson, five months; Elizabeth Coggin, three months; Thomas Crosby, six months; Isaac Fawcitt, twelve months. There were seven year olds, ten year olds, a girl on the threshold of womanhood at fourteen, a son of real value and source of pride to his parents at twenty-four, and those in their prime in their thirties and forties who often left children bereft of a parent, spouses destitute and the wider family having to take the burden of extra mouths to feed as children were distributed amongst them.

Jane felt glad that the last resting places of her husband, son and daughter were in the old cemetery, but she had accepted that there was simply no room for more when she was told that Tamar would be interred in the churchyard of the newer building. She went through the events of Tamar's funeral in her mind.

'T' were not that different to t'others,' she concluded. 'Even if t' pulpit's lacking grace, t' vicar says t' same things wi' nowt but a change in t' names. We all know t' words of interment and how to behave.'

She gathered a posy of wild flowers, laid it beneath the headstone of her husband and children's grave and then made her way into Robin Hood's Bay.

Jane paused at Lingers Beck on the way into Bay Town to let her horse drink from the clear, cold water but, as soon as she entered that part of the village where steep inclines, uneven road surfaces and open gullies crossing the road made travel more problematic, she released the animal. She tethered it where there was a little grazing and walked down King Street to the Newton family butcher's shop. She was hot and tired and, although she had more liking for Bay Town than Whitby, she never felt comfortable amongst the closely packed buildings, the teeming life where children played in dirty, open drains and the smells of human activity permeated the air. She felt claustrophobic and missed the clean, fresh air of the moors, the space where youngsters could roam freely. She also missed the comfort of her own home where there was life aplenty, but where rooms were more spacious and smells were more the result of food preparation than Bay Town's constant pervasive smell of fish and its overcrowded population.

'T' railway might be bringing in visitors to the town,' she puzzled, 'but what these townsfolk expect to see when they get here, I don't know. They'd be better off staying at home. Bay Town's nowt but fit for fisher folk. T' scenery might be nice for these artistic ones, but they'd not be so enthusiastic if they had to live here.'

She hoped that young Henry's father would be around to offer her a cup of tea. She had brought a token of respect, a bunch of her best lavender, for the poor man had lost his wife to a fever within the year and she knew he missed her, despite the ministrations of his wider family.

'They're good folk,' she thought. 'Just like the rest on us, takin' in Philip and Mary all those years ago when their mother died, and now t' brother-in-law and young Jane when there was more death in t' family. And I've nothing against young Henry or his family, for their hearts lie in the land, but I want to know his intentions towards my Margaret.'

The Newtons' butchery faced on to the street. Sawdust drifted across the road and blood from the carcasses stained the surrounding area. Henry himself was inside the premises when she arrived. Wrapped in a huge, bloodstained apron, he was manhandling sides of pork and lamb onto hooks screwed to the ceiling beams. He had strong working arms and hands, stained but scrubbed. His body was solidly built and obviously used to manual labour. His face was that of a kind man with smile lines and a gentle countenance.

Jane liked Henry, and she liked his family. They were honest; they did not sell the carcasses of sheep that had died, only those they had slaughtered. They did not pollute their sausages with sawdust or sweepings as some butchers did. They were thrifty, 'Nose-to-tail butchery,' Jane called it. Not a single element of an animal went to waste; black pudding, sausages, brains, hearts, sweetbreads, liver, kidney, bones and pluck (the lungs and intestines of sheep) were sold alongside expensive joints, gammon, bacon, chicken, rabbit, hare and game.

The Newtons had a smallholding and, in Jane's opinion, farmers did not put the time, effort and money into rearing animals to waste any of their products. She was often in awe of the remarkable range that they sold but the Pickerings bought none of their wares. They produced their own meat, and the women of the house were adept at making meals from every part of an animal by creating everything from pies, pastries, stews, black puddings, sausages and potted meats to roasts, boiled bacons and meat rolls.

Henry immediately offered her tea in the shade of the kitchen at the back of the shop. She joined him in the usual pleasantries, but as soon as there was a lull in the conversation, she did what she always did and came straight to the point.

She had come on a special mission. She'd given the matter a great deal of thought and she'd come to the conclusion (the same conclusion she always came to when dealing with delicate matters) that honesty was the best policy. Unskilled in diplomacy and uncomfortable with nuance, she said, 'Now, young Henry, hast tha' got an eye for my Margaret?'

Henry knew Jane well. He liked her down-to-earth approach to life and he liked her lack of guile. Even so, he found the words to reply to this straight question difficult. 'I like the girl a lot,' he mumbled. 'She's a fine lass.'

'Does tha' intend to ask her to wed thee?'

Again, Henry mumbled as he tried to reply. 'I've a mind to, but I'm not sure she'll have me. And I'm not sure of your blessing, Mrs Pickering. You need help wi' t' new bairns in t' house and I'll not deprive little ones of a mother's care. Margaret's like a mother to 'em, just as you are. I canna' tek from those who've lost already.'

'You're a good man, Henry. You speak sense. But Margaret's older 'n you and there's some fine lasses'd tek to thee – lasses o' child-bearing age. Why Margaret? She'll not give thee a family, and she'll not give thee an heir to thy inheritance. She's of that age where a woman's no longer going to be a mother. Don't speak well o' t' lass and then find another. I'll not let my daughter be the plaything of any man.'

'I'm not that kind of man, Mrs Pickering.'

'That's a truth I believe, and tha' seems fond o' t' lass. She's a good girl and tha'd be a lucky man to get her Henry Newton. We'll have to think on it, but I'm not minded to stand in her way. She's been mother to so many and housewife for me, but never had a husband of her own. I'll not manage wi'out t' girl if I'm honest, but it'd be a fine mess if she misses t' chance of a life wi' thee, if that's what she's about. But it'll be a fine mess for me if she teks that chance.'

'There's a conundrum,' said Henry. 'Where's t' answer?'

They sat in silence, Jane with her thoughts of trying to cope without Margaret, Henry unsure of how to suggest an answer to the problem. Jane broke the silence first. 'Tha' needs must talk to Margaret, Henry. Let her think on her own future. But it'll be a big change in our lives you'll be causing. Think on, man. Think on.'

Henry looked crestfallen but also relieved. Jane had not rejected his suit, and he wanted to tell Margaret about his feelings for her. He understood the problem; he simply did not know the solution.

Jane saw Henry's father, John, before she left and greeted the rest of the family. John was looking frail and all of his seventy-six years, but the difference to John if Henry left the home would not be as great as if Margaret left her. John's granddaughter would care for him. Jane did not have a replacement for Margaret, and she considered Thorney Brow a far greater commitment than the Newtons' shop. She was glad she'd spoken to Henry, but she was apprehensive about the future.

Jane returned to Thorney Brow after her visit to Bay Town. It was later than she had intended because of her diversion to St Stephen's Church, and the light was failing. Streaks of red on the western horizon gave promise of another fine day, but Jane had listened to the birds in the shrubs and hedgerows, watched the water out to sea as white horses played on the surface, and seen cattle in the fields grow restless; she knew that there was the likelihood of a storm. She twitched the whip against her horse and urged it to move a little faster.

As it trotted along a route that was so familiar it needed no guidance from her, Jane pondered the future. She would be a mother to her grandchildren; she would be the rock on which they and her youngest son would depend. She would strive to give them a future and help them grow to love the land that gave them succour. She had faced challenges before and she would face these new challenges. Henry Newton would marry Margaret. Gowan's children would be safe. Gowan had repeatedly said that one day he would reunite his family but, until that time, Jane would be there for him.

But she was also a realist. She knew she was no longer that young mother who had taken on Thorney Brow when her husband had died. She knew her time for being mother to infant children was running short. 'There's only one thing obvious right now,' she thought. ''Tis Gowan who's in need of a new wife. In fact, Gowan's more in need of a wife than Margaret's in need of a husband! T' poor lad looks a shadow of himself, but give him time and he'll find someone.'

She felt more comfortable about the future by the time she reached Thorney Brow. Two questions were settled: Margaret would get a husband, and Gowan would get a wife, possibly with a little help from herself. She had made up her mind, and Jane liked to have a positive mind.

As she approached the house and heard the sound of children's voices carrying across the land, she prayed that God would be with her as she and her family faced a new future, and that He would give back to her and her grandchildren the son and father that they had known. The future would present challenges, but Jane also thanked God for her own good health, her family's support and the blessing of this glorious, unforgiving, harsh but beautiful land.

FOUR

JANE PICKERING DISLIKED the prospect of visiting Whitby, yet fate decreed that periodically a visit was necessary. Today was such a day. She polished her boots and put on her best black-silk dress, the one reserved for funerals, weddings and important visits. She tied her now grey hair into a neat bun and wrapped her black woollen shawl around her shoulders.

From the station at Whitby, she made her way purposefully to Baxtergate where she found the address she was looking for; the shining brass plate at the side of the door announced it to be the offices of Buchannan and White: Solicitors.

A smartly dressed young man greeted her and told her that Mr White would be available shortly. True to his word, the young man returned quickly from the rear of the premises, told her that Mr White would be happy to see her now, and ushered her into a large, well-appointed study. A richly woven carpet, maroon-painted walls adorned with oil paintings and a fine fire-place with a tapestry screen were the backdrop for a substantial desk, three solid wood and leather chairs, and a bookcase containing legal texts. Mr White rose from his seat, greeted her and indicated that she should sit on one of the chairs opposite his at the desk.

Robert White was a competent solicitor. He was forty-four years old, lived in Ruswarp with his wife and three children, and had been recruited by the senior partner, George Buchannan, when the railway had brought sufficient business into Whitby to require another legal practitioner. The firm had dealt with the

Pickering family for many years – their wills, the occasional disputes that resulted from their farming practices, their tenancies and their business interests – so Mr White was well-acquainted with Jane and the wider Pickering family. He enquired after her health, expressed his condolences at the loss of her daughter-in-law and asked how he could help.

To Jane, the room seemed claustrophobic, the air stuffy with a hint of beeswax, the necessity of talking about family matters to an outsider uncomfortable. She wanted the interview to be as brief as possible. Her accustomed directness served her well on this occasion, and she briefly outlined her concerns.

'As tha' knows, we'd drawn up a tenancy for my son Gowan to take over Thorney Brow so that I could retire. Now, I canna' retire. T' bairns need me, and Gowan's a real worker but he canna' be mother and father. That tenancy is no longer possible, and we'll need to put it back to me. But there's further complications. I'm minded of my daughter, Margaret, and young Mr Newton. They want to marry. I'll not stand in t' lass's way but I've decided I need her help too much to let her leave. My thought is that she can marry t' lad but they'll have to live at Thorney Brow. That way, Margaret helps with t' bairns and Henry Newton gets a wife but – and this is my concern – I'll not have a Newton tek the farm. If I meet my maker, I want Gowan to be sure of his inheritance and that his lads can take his place if, God forbid, anything happened to him.'

Robert White listened attentively. He had found, sometimes to his cost, that Jane's grasp of business, her dedication to her family, and her formidable intellect were not to be underestimated. He needed to clarify her legal position, but he did not want to offend her by treating her in the same way as he treated many of the women who sought his advice. Usually at this juncture, he would have suggested to some of them that they brought with them a male relative to ensure that they understood his advice, or that they entrusted their dealings with the law to a father, brother or son. That was certainly not the way to deal with Jane Pickering!

He decided to risk her wrath by reiterating some of the points she would need to consider, but he knew that, if a decision were to be made, it would be Jane who made it.

'Bear with me, Mrs Pickering,' he said, 'whilst I put your thoughts into their legal framework, for I think there is a need to consider a wider picture before any decisions are made. As you know, the Pickerings do not own all the land they use. Your landlords are the Dinsdale family of Durham, a noble family that can trace its roots back to the days of the Norman Conquest and probably beyond. But the Pickering family is favoured because the marriage of John Hodgson, of Dinsdale descent, into the Pickering line has given you favourable terms of tenure.

'However, I must point out to you that the Dinsdales have fallen on hard times over the past years and the terrible crash of the New York stock market this year has added further problems. Therefore, I suggest you consider two possible outcomes. One is that the Dinsdales, regardless of filial loyalties, will need to increase your rents; the other is that you consider offering to buy some or all of their land that you farm, or that you consider offering to buy Thorney Brow. As you know, Mrs Pickering, your farming incomes have been healthy and your connections to the Dinsdales are close. As sitting tenants, you might well be favourably received. Such a move would, of course, give you much greater freedom over the use to which you put the land and decisions you make regarding who occupies the farm houses.'

Jane gave the poor man a withering look, straightened her back, took a deep breath, and replied. 'I'll thank thee, sir, to refrain from talking about my income. That is between me and my bank manager. And as for your lecture on our tenure and the Dinsdales, I think I'm pretty well acquainted with the situation. Tha'll need to concentrate on my daughter, Margaret, and my son, Gowan, if you please.'

Mr White blushed, wishing he had not bothered with a potted history of the Pickering's land tenure, and decided that he had better address the immediate issues rather than risk a further dressing down. 'I'm sorry if I offended you, dear lady,' he said, and promptly realised that Jane was not inclined to regard 'dear lady' as an acceptable form of address.

This interview was not going as well as he had hoped, but he battled on. 'Let us consider your daughter's proposed nuptials. Your suggestion that the couple live with you at Thorney Brow sounds an excellent solution to the problem. May I suggest that you ensure Margaret is catered for in the unhappy event of your demise by enshrining a bequest in your Will that provides for her future? This bequest could be offered in the form of a trust which could not be accessed by her husband but which might revert to the family should she predecease him? Would that put your mind at rest?'

Jane thought for a minute. 'Good,' she said. 'I think I'd be happy with that. Now, what about Gowan?'

'Gowan still lives at Browside, does he?'

'Yes.'

'But you would want him to have Thorney Brow if anything happened to you?'

'Yes.'

'A simple problem to solve. I suggest that your Will makes it clear that the tenancy for Thorney Brow is to be Gowan's. You are fortunate, for the Dinsdales have always allowed you to determine your own use of the tenancies. Giving your sons the name "Hodgson" after their Christian names perhaps has helped to ensure this latitude in their dealings with you. I see no problem with giving Gowan the right to continue farming the land. Possibly the greatest problems will be faced by the next generation, because they cannot all inherit. Like others, they will have to find work away from the land.'

'I canna' see my family away from t' land,' puzzled Jane. 'The land is our life. But I suppose you speak sense, Mr White, even if tha' knows little of farming. My family are proud of the name Hodgson but it doesna mek the land any bigger or more fertile. My sons John and William have their own tenancies and Gowan will have Thorney Brow, but none of the holdings'll support all the Pickering children of the next generation. T'will be a sad day if they leave, but I canna' be responsible for that. All I can do is mek sure my own children are catered for. We'll prepare a new Will. I'll speak to Margaret about young Henry Newton so that you can set up a trust for the girl, and we'll revert to the old tenancy for Thorney Brow until I'm no longer needed there. I thank you, Mr White.'

'I'll prepare the documents and let you know when they're ready for you to approve then, Mrs Pickering.' Mr White proffered his hand. Jane shook it and he ushered her out of his office.

Outside the solicitor's office, Jane breathed a sigh of relief. 'T' man means well and he might know the law, but he's no concept o' farming,' she muttered. 'Trouble is, he's right. Our land'll never support all of William, John and Gowan's boys. I'll need to think on that. But it's good to be out of that stuffy office.'

She made her way down Baxtergate towards St Ann's Staith. Her route took her past the bank where she needed to see her bank manager. As a known and valued customer, she did not have long to wait. Mr Chambers welcomed her into his office and, as had Mr White, enquired after her health and offered his condolences.

Having placed a large folder of papers in front of himself, he congratulated her on her careful handling of the farm's business. Jane waved aside his remarks and pointed out that the purpose of her visit was to revoke her instruction to him to purchase a property for her retirement. 'I'll not be able to put me feet up yet!' she remarked. 'But I'll need to mek sure t' money's kept safe for t' future.'

Despite her misgivings about the railway, Jane had to admit that the monster had brought advantages beyond the obvious improvement of the access to Whitby and Scarborough. They had built the line on a section of land that she farmed. As a result, she now owned shares in the railway company and had also received compensation in the form of cash, which she had intended to use as payment for a new home in Hawsker. Bearing in mind Mr White's remarks, she asked the bank manager for an estimate of the value of the land which she farmed but which belonged to the Dinsdales.

His reply was not encouraging. 'Mrs Pickering, we've known each other for some time now, and you know I hold you in high esteem, but to finance both the ventures you are suggesting is out of the question. I regret having to talk of delicate matters, madam, but you are of an age when it is difficult to find lenders prepared to take the risk without asking for extortionate returns. Currently, you do not have sufficient assets to purchase both the Dinsdales' land and a property for your own use. That means retirement would be problematic if you wanted to live away from Thorney Brow.'

Jane liked Mr Chambers and appreciated his straight talking. She could see the wisdom of his advice. She briefly considered his words and reviewed her options.

'T' new laws giving women rights over their property might seem helpful to some, Mr Chambers, but t' law helps me not at all. T' world sees me as an old woman and favours t' young men when it comes to lending and borrowing funds. I'm blessed wi' sons who will care for t' land and perhaps it's their heritage to tek t' Dinsdales' land. You and I'll mek sure they can do it.

'But I appreciate your sagacity regarding the current handling of surplus funds. Tell me, Mr Chambers, there is much talk of uncertainty in the Stock Market. I feel it is an American problem for an Englishman would never be so foolish as to take the sort of risks that appear to have caused the problems that now beset New York. But would you advise investment in property as a better risk than shares in the current climate? I might not be in a financial position to consider buying both land and property, but my son Gowan has done well. He has begun a new venture transporting goods from the Flask Inn to Whitby, and I am minded to suggest to him that he considers making the Dinsdales an offer for Thorney Brow.'

Mr Chambers listened carefully to Jane's words, and his reply did not surprise her. 'I regret, madam, that I cannot discuss your son's finances with you, any more than I can discuss yours with him. You will need to talk to him yourself about his financial position. But I have two suggestions. First, that you continue to farm your land and care for your family, but that you retain control of assets. At some time in the future, possibly when your son takes over from you, they may be of sufficient value to help purchase either the Dinsdales' land or Thorney Brow. The second is that the surplus cash that you intended to use to purchase a retirement property could still be used for that purpose. Go ahead with the purchase, but rent it out until the day comes when you want it yourself. As your financial advisor, I have to put to you the current thinking in financial circles where land and property are being seen favourably as a secure investment.'

'I thank ye, sir. Tha's a good man. Tha' knows I'd set my heart on a little house for my retirement. I'd like you to arrange for its purchase and, when it's done, I'll take thy suggestion on board and find a tenant. And I'll tell my son to see you regarding the ownership of Thorney Brow, for it looks like it'll be for him to raise the money for Dinsdales' land and property.'

Jane left the bank feeling purposeful. In her heart of hearts, she knew that to borrow extensively at that moment in time would not be prudent, but she delighted in the power that her control of her finances gave her. She also revelled in the reflected glory of the compliments paid to Gowan regarding his most recent enterprise.

One day she would move to Hawsker, where Glenean had caught her eye as a suitable place to retire. It was a solidly built detached house with glorious views across the moors and a usable outside space for vegetables and chickens. Meanwhile, she would continue to do what she did best and manage the farm, its finances, and her family.

Her business was not quite complete; she never visited Whitby without ensuring that anything she needed from the town was dealt with on the same day, thus obviating the need for a return trip. She walked along Bridge Street as it crossed the Esk and joined the crowds that flocked to the market, the workshops, or their homes and places of business.

Here she found a tea shop and sat inside the tiny room refreshing herself with a pot of tea and a slice of parkin before continuing her mission. She was unimpressed. Tiny Georgian glazed windows let in little light, and the room was cramped. The only furnishings were two small round tables and six ill-assorted chairs that wobbled on the uneven flagstone floor. Water was obtained from a communal tap in the marketplace and heated on a kitchen range at the rear of the room, and the tiny lady, who appeared to be both proprietor and waitress, looked exhausted. Yet, Jane had to admit, the tea was well-brewed in a pretty china pot and was served in a delicate china cup with matching saucer, sugar bowl and milk jug. The slice of parkin had a pleasant taste of ginger, treacle, syrup and oatmeal, and the serviette matched the embroidered white tablecloth.

Jane guessed that this was the lady's living room and that the ladder at the side of the room led to a bedroom above. She felt a pang of sympathy for her hostess; to live and work in cramped, uncomfortable conditions and yet produce good food and drink was praiseworthy. But to Jane, not only the tearoom was anathema, but also the whole noisy, smelly, crowded scene.

She peered through the cloudy panes of glass and wished she were elsewhere. She gazed at the individuals who made up the heaving mass of humanity that passed by. A sad-looking figure walking with the aid of a crutch and with bandages encasing his legs shuffled past. He was probably not into his thirties and yet he walked like an old man, a horrible reminder of the vicious toll on life caused by Britain's involvement in the Boer War. To Jane, this was more an indication of the stupid arrogance and aggression of the male of the species than a dent in the nation's pride that the campaigns were lately being viewed as.

A small boy dodged in and out of the throng, his bare feet calloused, but his limbs agile and his eager eyes seeming to absorb the scene with a disarming familiarity. His clothing was little more than rags and he was heading towards the south-eastern part of the town where the Whitby Poor Law Union operated their workhouse. Jane guessed he should have been at the workhouse school, but she could not determine his age because workhouse children were notoriously small for their ages.

It reminded her of the good fortune that her involvement with the land endowed. When her own daughter-in-law had died, there had been no thought that the children would go to the workhouse. True to tradition, the family took on the extra burden.

'Imagine the shame!' thought Jane. 'And imagine those poor bairns leaving the land for life in a place like this!'

A solidly built woman with a basket of washing was chatting with another; they appeared to be comparing their work. Jane found their size amusing because both were larger than she and either Mary Ann or Margaret combined. At least those two were well-fed, she reassured herself, but they did not impress her with their apparel. Considering their occupation, they had precious little regard for personal hygiene. Yet again, the discrepancy between her own life, where cleanliness was highly regarded, and the lives of these town dwellers was only too obvious.

Two figures attracted Jane's attention. They stood directly in front of the teashop, one a young woman, plain looking, dark-haired, not fashionably dressed but clad in rather unkempt but serviceable boots and a tweed skirt and jacket. The other was a young girl, pretty, slightly built and dark haired, wearing a nicely made blue dress with a matching ribbon in her hair and well-polished boots. But it was not only their clothing or the strange mixture of contrasts and similarities that attracted Jane's attention, it was the fact that the young woman was wheeling a bicycle.

Jane gazed at her in horror. She had been told of an advertisement at the station in Scarborough that urged the reader to sell his horse and buy a bicycle, and she had seen men riding the machines along the main road that ran beyond Low Flask farm where William and his family lived. The innkeeper at the Flask Inn had even remarked that he did quite a good trade serving cyclists with food and drink. She believed that well-to-do women sometimes bought the things, but here was a young woman not only using a bicycle but possibly encouraging an innocent little girl to do the same!

Jane finished her tea, paid the woman who had served her and headed towards the market. She wanted to buy fabric and knew of a market stall where the trader charged a fair price and would keep whatever she ordered until either Gowan or William could collect it when they were next in Whitby. She found the stall, chatted briefly to the trader about the undoubted quality of black bombazine as a sturdy, reliable textile appropriate for all ages and all occasions, ordered a half roll and then made her way up the steep incline of Church Street towards St Mary's Church to make her last purchase of the day.

Even a stranger could have located Jane's final destination with little trouble. The Pickerings did not like fish – their diet was meat based – but they did like kippers occasionally, and whenever she visited Whitby, Jane took some back for the family as a treat.

The smoke houses belched smoke across the higher reaches of Church Lane and Henrietta Street and she could smell the comparatively pleasant aroma as she approached them. Inside the one she favoured, rows of gutted herring were hanging on poles gradually turning from grey to golden brown as the oak smoke preserved, flavoured and coloured them. She selected twelve of the most succulent and watched as the young boy given the responsibility of serving her wrapped them carefully in newspaper and put them into her shopping basket. Then she left, intending to head back to the station and catch the next train home.

It was as she arrived back at St Ann's Staith that Jane saw the young woman with the bicycle again. The little girl still accompanied her but, to Jane's surprise, they were heading purposefully towards the Mission to Seamen located at the beginning of Haggersgate.

'Hardly a suitable place for a little girl,' thought Jane. 'That young woman with the bicycle is responsible for this, I'll be bound. No self-respecting parent would allow a child, especially a pretty little thing like that, to go near a house dedicated to the ruffians who go to sea.'

Jane was fascinated. Instead of turning left to make her way back to the station, she turned right to watch them. This made her feel uncomfortable and her discomfort led her to imagine that she, too, was being watched.

She decided to give the impression that she had intended to walk towards Pier Road and set off in that direction, giving her imaginary stalker no reason to think that she was doing anything she had not intended to do. Unfortunately, the herring fleet was in and this route took Jane directly to the place where the herring girls worked. She understood nothing of their language, for they followed the herring fleet down the coast from their homes in Scotland and spoke Gaelic, but she did not need a qualification in linguistics to recognise the bawdy nature of their conversations and songs.

She watched entranced as the girls worked at lightning speed, flour sacking wound around their hands and wrists to protect them from accident as they used their sharp knives to gut the fish. Each girl was part of a team and used the same table as others in her group. They took the herring from a barrel where it was preserved in brine, gutted it, dropped the guts into a trough-like container at their feet and threw the fish into another barrel to be taken away for sale.

Jane tried to count. 'Unbelievable,' she muttered. 'Thirty herring a minute, I've been told, and that seems about right.'

The girls' bare feet slipped on mud, blood and guts, and their clothes were covered in the same mixture. The headscarves that tied their hair out of the way were little better. Jane had heard that the herring girls found it difficult to find lodgings in the town, and she was not surprised.

She decided to return to the Staith. As she passed the place where she had seen the mysterious young lady with the bicycle, she saw that same machine propped against a wall. She wasn't sure whether the owner had gone into the Mission for Seamen or the house next door. There was no sign of either the bicycle owner or of the little girl, but there was a notice outside the Mission to Seamen inviting anyone who cared to join in to enter the building for an afternoon piano recital.

Jane hesitated. A visit to Whitby was undoubtedly something to be avoided. Had she not seen enough filth, smelled enough fish, mixed with enough crowds, suffered enough claustrophobia for one day? And was it not time to head back to Thorney Brow? The pot of tea and slice of parkin had had barely satisfied her growing hunger, and Margaret would be preparing the evening meal very shortly. But a piano recital was different; it showed a side of Whitby of which she knew nothing, and she was encouraged by the sight of several women, clean and sensibly dressed, entering the building. That suggested the concert was aimed at a different clientele from the sailors to whom it was dedicated.

She asked one of the women how long the recital was likely to last and was told that it would be an hour at the most, but that she was free to leave at any time if she so wished.

Apprehensively, Jane entered the building and took a seat at the back, reasoning that she could make a quick and discreet exit if she wanted to. The room was plain, save for various prints and paintings of ships that adorned the walls. Chairs were arranged in rows facing a raised platform on which a piano was set slightly to one side, allowing room for either a preacher or speaker or even a small choir.

A man in traditional fisherman's clothing – navy-blue trousers, dark-navy jumper, neckerchief and heavy fisherman's boots, rose and took the stage. He thanked the audience for their attendance and reminded them that there was a collecting box at the entrance; all donations would be used for the relief of seamen and their families who needed support. He then announced that a young lady with whom he felt they were familiar would give the afternoon's recital. As he beckoned to an individual sitting at the front of the gathering, Jane felt a tingling sensation of shock. The individual he summoned was none other than the girl in the blue dress who had attracted her attention earlier.

'May I present Miss Lily Booth,' he announced.

'T' lass canna' be more 'n eleven or twelve years old!' Jane murmured to herself as the audience clapped.

A voice beside responded to Jane's muttered outburst. 'She's a talented lass, she is, and no mistake. Have ye not seen her before?'

'I've not been here before,' replied Jane. 'I live out on Fylingdales.'

'Well tha's in for a treat,' her neighbour said. 'She's t' youngest of the Booth girls and a fine musician. Her sister's a teacher. Ye might know her – I think she works somewhere near you, at Howdale Moor.'

Music from the piano ended their conversation. Jane sat entranced; music was not part of her life. Young girls were expected to learn womanly skills such as cooking, cleaning, sewing, dairy work, poultry work. In Jane's world, they were never likely to encounter a piano, and most certainly not expected to expose themselves to public scrutiny! Yet the sound of the music mesmerised her, as did the the sight of a young girl holding an audience in thrall and the knowledge that the teacher who was responsible for her grandchildren's education was part of the same family as this talented child.

When the concert ended, Jane put a contribution in the box at the entrance to the building and emerged into the noise and hubbub of Whitby life. She made her way to the station and caught the train, but she saw little of the scenery that flashed by as she travelled home. Her mind was full of images of the little girl in the blue dress, and she was struggling to cope with the idea that families could educate girls to do more than work as housekeepers and farmers.

Gowan had hoped that Reginald would go to Whitby Grammar School, but the boy had shown little interest and preferred to work with his beloved horses. Jane had never seen the point of educating Reginald further for, as she had pointed out, 'Horses need a firm hand, not a book!'

None of the other boys had shown any particular liking for school, except young Gowan who was said to be an intelligent lad. As for the girls…

Jane wondered why she had not put two and two together. Lily Booth was the sister of the teacher at Howdale School; that meant the Booth family had encouraged their daughters to look beyond the confines of the home for their futures. Not only that, the Booth girls had not taken up the usual forms of employment available to girls and become maids, charwomen, laundresses or, God forbid, ladies of the night.

'Why would they do that?' she deliberated. 'A girl needs to marry. What use is an ability to play music when there's a home to run and bairns that need caring for? No girl can take up employment if she marries. That Booth family might be talented, but they've little common sense. Possibly a life in Whitby is so different to a life on the moors that young lasses get to do things that are beyond our ken.'

Yet, despite her mixed emotions, Jane's visit to Whitby had been worthwhile. She had ensured the continuity of Thorney Brow as a home and source of income for Gowan and his children, solved the problem of Margaret's marriage to Henry Newton and ended her dilemma about her future retirement.

That evening the family enjoyed a supper of kippers, and Margaret learned that she had her mother's blessing to her marriage, providing the couple lived at Thorney Brow. Margaret accepted the prospect as a good solution to a problem she was well aware of.

Jane was still pondering Mr White's opinion that all the land they farmed might one day belong to them, but that it was inadequate to support them all. No matter how much she consoled herself with the thought that her male grandchildren were not her concern, she worried about their futures. And no matter how she tried to exorcise the picture of the little girl in the blue dress from her mind, the vision kept returning, forcing her to consider that the new century might hold the prospect of women looking for more than a life dedicated to home making.

FIVE

FRAN STOOD ON the platform of the station at Fyling Hall and waited excitedly for the train from Whitby to arrive. It was August, and the weather was glorious. There were beautiful blue skies above fields where there were the golden remains of the harvest not yet gathered. A gentle swell disturbed an almost still sea, and a skylark hovered above, its persistent call contrasting with the erratic screams of a herring gull.

Noise from an approaching train disturbed the scene; its engine roared, smoke belched, sparks flew, steam hissed, pistons clanked. A gloved hand waved from the window of one of its carriages, and the familiar sight of Ada Robertson came into view. Fran waved back.

The train drew to a slow, noisy stop, and the door of Ada's carriage opened. She struggled with a small, but apparently heavy, suitcase as she alighted onto the platform. The two young women greeted each other with a hug. Ada gazed eagerly about her. She was small and petite, and her sandy hair and blue eyes contrasted with Fran's dark hair and brown, almost black, eyes.

'At last!' an elated Fran greeted her friend. 'Now you'll see my little domain. And you'll love it as much as I do. We'll have such fun together and you'll learn more about country ways. Have you brought your watercolours? I see you took my advice and put on your sturdy footwear. We'll explore. We'll visit the places I have spoken of so often, and you will meet the people you've only heard about. Oh, Ada! This will be a splendid holiday.'

Fran's obvious delight was matched by Ada's enthusiasm as the latter's eyes sparkled and a wide smile lit her radiant face.

William Petty was waiting outside the station with the farm cart. The girls boarded the cart and set off for Brow, where Fran had come to an agreement that Ada would share her room at the Petty family's farm where she lodged during school term time. Their long-planned holiday had begun.

As the farm cart plodded towards Brow, Ada gazed at the landscape. Fran had described the scene so often, told of the people who wrenched a living from the land and of their ways. They were very different to the inhabitants of Whitby, where Ada, like Fran, was a teacher.

Ada admired her friend. She knew it was hard enough being responsible for youngsters without the added burden of working single handedly, and without the extra problems created by a lack of basic amenities. It did not surprise her that Fran spent all her leisure time in Whitby. The holiday they were about to have together would be almost as much a learning experience for Fran as it was for herself. It would be a voyage of discovery for them both.

The timing of Fran and Ada's holiday had been chosen to coincide with the start of the grouse shooting season. During a visit to Howdale School, the local curate had suggested that Fran would enjoy the spectacle of a grouse shoot and encouraged her to become a foot follower for the special occasion of the 12th of August. This was the day when not only grouse shooting could begin here on Fylingdales, but hunting went into full swing. Huntsmen could now follow adult foxes instead of just cubs, and deer stalking was extended to include stags.

The people of Fylingdales knew the Scots referred to this day as the 'Glorious Twelfth'. When Fran told Ada that they could be part of the event, her friend's Scottish roots ensured a joyful response – although, as Ada pointed out, she was an Aberdonian, not a Highlander.

The two young women had laughed at the apparent inconsistency of the School Board, which had appointed Ada as one of their teachers. They had prided themselves on their appointment of a Scot, for they held the Scottish educational system in high esteem, yet, as Ada pointed out, she was a product of the same town that supplied the herring girls amongst whom that system appeared to have had little impact!

Their first thoughts on arriving at the Petty's cottage were of the coming shoot, but that evening they took a stroll along the path to Howdale School so that Ada could see it first hand. She was impressed. Its vantage point, set above a drop down to pasture land where cows and horses grazed, gave an uninterrupted view of the sea which glimmered in the evening air. A boat at anchor appeared like a toy at that distance, but implied life even in the depths of the ocean. Birds chattered in the rough hedgerows; the evening flight of swallows gorging on insects gave life to the air, and the hoot of an owl as darkness approached told of scurrying rodents.

The ground behind the school rose steeply. Rough bracken, hawthorn, wild lilac and small saplings bent almost double against the wind were the foreground to a sky that was turning pink. It promised a fine day for the shoot.

'We have had so many adventures together, Fran,' remarked Ada. 'Think of our train rides to York or to Scarborough to see where the pier had stood before it was washed away in a storm. And our holidays with your father's friends at Kirkby Moorside, or our train rides to Goathland, Grossmont, Egton Bridge, Runswick Bay and Staithes. But this has got to be a highlight for me. You may be accustomed to such beauty on your doorstep, but I find it truly inspiring. You asked if I had brought my watercolours. I think it would be outside my compass to capture what I am looking at on canvas or paper! You are so lucky – you see

48

this every day.' The two friends had spent many happy hours together and formed a strong friendship, and their good health and sturdy young legs had allowed them to explore the wider world.

Fran was silent for a moment. She had forgotten that this landscape had first affected her in the same way as it was now affecting her friend. She had grown used to it, and she was conscious of the adage 'familiarity breeds contempt'. Was she taking it for granted, immune to its grandeur? Was she so engrossed in the daily routine of school, travelling to and from Whitby and enduring the inconveniences of life here on the moors that she had forgotten the magnificence of what was in front of her every day?

'You serve as a salutary reminder, Ada,' she said. 'I thought that our joint venture into my little world would lead me to a better understanding of my pupils – I thought that their rural backgrounds were something I need to learn more about. But you have just reminded me of why I fell in love with this harsh place when I first came here. Thank you, Ada. No matter what the future holds for us, I must always remember that this is a very special place – and I will attribute that understanding to you.'

The two young women linked arms and made their way back to their lodgings. Fran felt a fresh wave of love for her second home, and Ada was excited that the next day would bring more delights.

◆ ◆ ◆

Tuesday 12th August dawned bright and sunny. Ada and Fran set out from their lodgings at Brow, climbed the steep incline towards the moors where the shoot was assembling, and joined a group of others who were also heading to the wide acreages of open ground. Both the young women wore straw hats, simple cotton blouses and light skirts, unencumbered by the heavy petticoats of winter.

Once they reached the highest point, the vista opened out before them. Unkempt sheep nibbled at sparse leafy foliage. Cotton grass released clumps of wispy down into the air, and the ubiquitous heather spread across the vast landscape interspersed only with bracken and as yet unripe bilberries.

But it was not a landscape bereft of people, for the start of the grouse-shooting season had brought people from every direction. Horses and carriages, rough farm carts, individuals on horseback and others on foot were all assembling at the place where butts gave a vantage point for marksmen. The butts were arranged at a sufficient distance from each other to ensure their occupants could cover wide swathes of ground. They were semi-circles of dry-stone walls inside which earth had been hollowed out and piled up to give the marksmen a base on which they could steady their sights. They were so much a part of the landscape that an unaware visitor may well have missed them.

Fran and Ada met the Martindale family of Cook House. Fran introduced her friend to William Martindale who, in turn, introduced them to other participants of the shoot: Thomas Newton, who was staying with his in-laws, the Harlands of Spring Hill; Matthew Brewster of Mill Beck Lane; John Newton, another relative of the Harland family, and William and Gowan Hodgson Pickering. Fran had little need of the introductions for she was known to them all having taught youngsters from each of their families, but they all expressed their pleasure and surprise that she had chosen to join them and seemed pleased that she had brought a 'town girl' with her.

The grouse marksmen were all male, and a few of the men were less than impressed with the women's presence because they viewed the sport as a male preserve. However, most of them made Fran and Ada feel welcome and went to considerable lengths to explain the technicalities of using their guns and to introduce them to their dogs, mainly springer spaniels and retrievers.

A few asked if the two young women intended to follow the hunt, and Fran and Ada decided they would. The Justice of the Peace John Barry's party impressed them most; whilst most of the shooting parties arrived on foot or in simple carts, he arrived in a well-appointed coach from his country house, Fyling Hall, with three guests, his stockman and his estate manager.

Large wicker baskets containing fine china, crystal glass, silver cutlery, wine, bread, meat, cheese and pastries were carried to a spot immediately behind where Ada and Fran had found a vantage point. Servants had cleared an area of heather and undergrowth and set up a collapsible table and chairs. Mr Barry opened a fine leather case brought to him by his estate manager and he and his guests admired the intricate carvings on the rifle it contained.

Mr Barry took his shooting stick to the nearest butt and, when he and his guests were assembled to their satisfaction, a signal was made. Wielding besoms, flags or sticks, youths (some barely more than children), farm workers, cattlemen, shepherds, stockmen and pigmen moved out from behind the butts to beat the earth, rattle the clumps of dry heather and, in the process, drive out the grouse from their hides on the ground up into the air.

Guns went off from every butt on that stretch of moorland as the marksmen enjoyed the challenge of shooting the rapidly flying birds. The noise was deafening and the speed of the entire event remarkable. A break in the firing while the marksmen reloaded their guns allowed the dogs to be released, and they ran out joyously to fetch the fallen birds. Within a short time, the whole process began again, this time with the beaters further from the butts.

Fran and Ada were entranced, dazed, deafened, excited, fascinated. 'Now we know why many followers of the shoot did not ride out on their horses, and why those who did made sure they had companions who could remove the animals from the scene,' remarked Ada. 'The poor creatures would have been terrified.'

'I can hardly believe the speed of the birds' flight, or the skill of the guns,' commented Fran.

After several rounds of shooting, the participants decided to take a break. The Barry party indulged in their beautifully prepared banquet whilst the others enjoyed a simpler repast of bread, cheese, cold meats, pickles, and drank cider or beer.

During the respite, several youngsters approached Fran. There was a 'Good afternoon, Miss Booth' from George and Richard Harland, and Reginald Pickering doffed his cap, proud that his old teacher was there to see his mastery of his newly acquired gun.

'Hello, Miss Booth. Are you liking the shoot?' asked young Gowan Pickering, with a twinkle in his eye and obvious delight contrasting as it always did with the embarrassment of his brother, John Clark, who politely pulled his forelock but remained mute.

Ada and Fran loved it all. To Ada, it was especially poignant as it brought back memories of her childhood in Scotland where stories of the 'Glorious Twelfth' abounded.

They had brought a picnic of bread and cheese, but were given cider and beer by some of the other spectators and asked to join a small shooting party organised by one of the Newton family. The sultry summer air, cooled only by a mild breeze from the sea and the excitement of the day, doubtless combined with the effects of the alcohol, left them slightly light-headed.

At the end of the day, after they had thanked their hosts for their hospitality, they made their way back to the Petty family home in a state of mild euphoria. They sang 'Camptown Races' and 'My Bonnie Lies Over the Ocean' to the amusement of other shoot followers who were leaving the scene. In deference to their hosts as they approached the Petty's home, they changed to the hymn 'Now the Day is Over' hoping a nod to propriety would impress. That night they slept well; their holiday had already exceeded their expectations.

Wednesday was another fine day, but they spent it more quietly. Ada dutifully took her watercolours to a vantage point looking towards Robin Hood's Bay and tried to capture the steep inclines of the town's road system and the assortment of roofing styles and shapes that characterised its architecture. She attempted a pretty blue wash as a background to fishing boats in the harbour, then a deep green stripe to replicate the contrast of foliage where rocky cliffs supported moss and lichen combined with shrubs and outcrops of sturdy, windswept trees.

Fran knew her limitations. Her life in the Booth family home had taught her that she was an adept needlewoman, but not an artist. She loved to watch her friend so preoccupied, however, and was full of praise for Ada's work. They reminisced about the previous day's events and conjectured about the forthcoming hunt.

'What did you think of Mr Barry and his party?' queried Fran.

'More money than sense!' came Ada's immediate response.

'I can't imagine living in that way, but I suppose it lets him to do more or less what he pleases,' Fran ruminated. 'I hear that Mr Barry's had a new pig sty constructed in the style of the Greek Parthenon. I can't believe that such a construction would benefit anyone, but perhaps it makes him feel very grand.'

Ada looked horrified. 'I see poverty all around me in Whitby. I see people living in hovels and children barely fed. Are his pigs of greater significance than his fellow man? Can't people with so much money do something to benefit mankind? I really feel I don't like Mr Barry, Fran. I despise the man.'

'Perhaps having so much wealth takes people away from reality,' Fran suggested. 'The wealthy seem to use a different yardstick for their measurement of need. Mr Barry's father was partly responsible for building the new St Stephen's Church, and he was praised for his donation. It was said that the Reverend Cooper complained that the three-decker pulpit in the Old St Stephen's Church towered in the middle of the box pews, many of which turned towards the pulpit rather than the chancel. This conflicted with his beliefs. He persuaded Mr Robert Barry, who was master of Fyling Hall at the time, to help with the costs of the new church. You and I were brought up in the Nonconformist church, Ada, and we have little understanding of the ways of Anglicans. Most of the farmers around here are keen Anglican supporters. Perhaps they're better placed to assess the worth of the Barrys than are we.'

'Well, I have my own thoughts,' concluded an affronted Ada. 'Will the Barrys be at the hunt tomorrow?'

Ada and Fran intended to follow the hunt on foot. Many of the local farmers were followers of the Staintondale Hunt and spent as much time as they could in August and September riding to hounds if they were wealthy enough to have stables of sufficient quality. If not, they followed on foot.

The riders spoke of the exhilaration of trekking, chasing, clearing walls and ditches and bogs on their mounts, following the most direct routes regardless of obstacles to be first at the kill. They enjoyed the comradeship of the hunters and hunt followers at the inns – the Falcon, Shepherd's Arms, Scalby Mills and Flask. They would return home after their days in the saddle with stories of the hunt, descriptions of the cliffs round Ravenscar and Robin Hood's Bay, of rocky outcrops at Maybeck, Falling Foss and Little Beck, and of the dangers of the bogs on the moorland across Fylingdales to Juggera, Brow Moor, Low Moor and Sneaton. On Sundays, when hunting was not permitted, they rested and tended their horses and dogs, preparing for the following week. They encouraged their sons to follow in their footsteps; hunting was a tradition of which they were proud.

The hunt assembled at the Flask Inn where the local farmers rode with their dogs, mostly hounds but some terriers, took a glass of gin and headed to Howdale Moor. Ada and Fran watched the riders head off to the moor and joined a substantial number of other foot followers.

At first the hounds picked up the scent of a dog fox but the animal went to ground in a drain and, despite some men putting their terriers down to fetch it out, it escaped. Past Cook House, they picked up a fresh scent and the horn sounded to let the riders know a chase was on. The hounds settled to their fox very quickly, and the field rode at full gallop across the rough ground. Each rider wanted to be first at the kill and claim the brush and mask but, as the distance grew, some took the lead.

The excitement of the race meant furious speed, a great deal of shouting and cheering, the noise of the horns, the barking of dogs and danger for all as dry stone walls were cleared, boggy patches of moor were trampled and farm animals scattered. Occasionally, women emerged from their cottages to remonstrate with the riders as they trampled vegetable patches, frightened cows and chickens and damaged fencing.

Foot followers brought up the rear. Many had stopped trying to keep up with the fast-moving hunt, but others, including Fran and Ada, persevered. A few ladies on ponies and well-presented horses trotted behind the main event, hoping to glimpse the final kill. This happened at Alison Head Wood and, breathless and with their legs aching, Fran and Ada were not long after the leaders arriving at the spot.

They sank onto a bank of soft bracken to rest. 'Well! What did you think to that?' Fran quizzed her friend.

'I was so excited by it – it was awe-inspiring. All that the speed, the hullabaloo, the magnificent horses! I've seen paintings of hunting scenes – they're very popular in a lot of parlours – but none do justice to the real thing. They don't capture the thrill of the chase, the noise, the exhilaration, the camaraderie of the riders or their skill.' Ada was entranced. 'But I didn't like to see the damage done by the recklessness of the event. I saw a poor woman weeping at the loss of some of her allotment.'

The discussion was brought to a halt by the arrival of several local farmers. Gowan Pickering was amongst them. 'What are thy thoughts on the hunt, Miss Booth?' he asked.

Fran blushed. To talk to this man in her schoolroom had always given her pleasure, but here, on what was obviously his territory, she did not expect him to address her. She hesitated and was about to reply to the effect that she very much enjoyed the hunt when he turned to Ada. 'And did our little sport please you, Miss Robertson?' he asked.

Fran felt rebuffed and rather silly. Fumbling, she pushed a stray lock of hair back and tried to appear unruffled as Ada replied, 'It did, sir. Yet, if I am to be honest, I was concerned at the damage that you do. Does the hunt recompense those who lose by its disruption?'

Gowan laughed. ''Tis my living that is damaged!' he exclaimed. 'I will compensate myself if it makes thee happier, Miss Robertson but I think tha' knows that my family farms all t' land as far as t' eye can see in these parts. I think I am master of how 'tis treated. The holders of t' small allotments will soon recover from the inconvenience. 'Tis my compensation for the toil that I and my family put into t' soil. Would thee rather a fox ate my chickens than I fed my bairns? Or deer destroy the grazing land? The hunt is enjoyable but 'tis also a necessity.'

Ada looked at Gowan uncertainly. In a somewhat sarcastic tone, she remarked, 'I am glad you so enjoy your work, sir.'

Gowan looked annoyed. 'T' Scots are masters of the shoot, and they seem to like it well enough. I hear tell that your fellow countryman, Mr Keir Hardy, made a fool of himself when he was first elected a Member of Parliament by presenting himself in tweeds and a deerstalker – yet he seemed to dislike landowners. Now Mr Campbell Bannerman wants to interfere with t' way we country folk live. I hope, Miss Robertson, that you are not a supporter of rabble-rousers like Mr Hardy and t' Liberals who would destroy the rights of men like me to take pleasure from their land. Does t' schoolroom never give you pleasure? Are t' children in your care no more than t' tools of your trade? And would thee have them starve if t' killing of t' vermin that tek their food gave pleasure to the hunter?'

Despite her earlier embarrassment Fran came to her friend's rescue, for she was afraid Ada's outspoken ways and sympathy with the Liberal cause, so welcomed by her own family, might be less than popular in present company. She drew a deep breath and interrupted. 'It is difficult to liken our work to yours, sir. But I think I speak for us both in saying that the children in our care give us immense pleasure. In my case, that pleasure derives in no small measure from your own children. I delighted to see that Reginald, John Clark and Gowan were amongst the followers of the shoot and the hunt, and my only sadness is that they cannot stay in my classroom for longer. I was saddened when Reginald left my schoolroom.'

'Reginald's a clever lad, Miss Booth, but he had no liking for learning. It's best that he should tek advantage of t' local authority's bylaws. They're meant to let lads like him work on t' land, and if they say he can gi' us t' help we need when he's turned twelve years old then we're not going to argue. But I thank you for your work wi' them all, for they like your little schoolroom and they learn well while they are there.'

Gowan's brother, William, joined them and the tension that had entered the conversation eased. Physically, the two men were very similar – tall, dark-haired and muscular. But William lacked Gowan's characteristic voice, which was mellow yet clear and, when necessary, loud and commanding. The two men gestured to the ground next to where the friends were sitting. In response to Fran's invitation to join them, they sat down.

'And dost thee have compliments for my children too, Miss Booth?' William laughed.

'I do indeed, sir! Between you and your brother, I am a busy person – and a contented one,' Fran was quick to reply.

'I believe you are a respected veterinary, Mr Pickering?'

'Veterinary, yes. Respected, not sure,' came the reply. 'Why, on t' first day o' t' shoot, I was talking to our doctor. He had made three calls that day and could do nothing for any of those poor sick people who asked for his help other than give morphine. I can set bones and help deliver new life, but I do not have the painful task of easing suffering in those for whom there is no cure. I trust my gun. The good doctor is well-respected. I am simply a country man wi' a love of animals.'

'And a good way wi' them, brother,' interjected Gowan. 'Many a farmer round here has been glad o' your services. Do you remember that time when you were called by a young lad to attend a cow wi' "dottylucas" and, when you arrived at t' farm, you found it was tuberculosis? The old man who owned the cow said he knew it was something like that! You not only shot his cow for him, but could tell him what tuberculosis was. I remember he was very grateful. Was that not t' same old chap who got stuck in his stirrups at t' hunt?'

'Nay, brother, that were Samuel from Littlebeck.' William chuckled at the recollection. 'T' old fella heard t' hunt while he was workin' in t' yard. So anxious was he not to miss a minute more than he had to, he jumped on his horse, galloped off t' moors. Only at t' end of t' day's ride, when he was at t' Falcon waiting on a glass, did he realise he'd still got his farm boots on. He couldna' get out of t' stirrups! We had to cut him out!'

William and Gowan laughed at the recollection and Fran and Ada found their laughter infectious. Shortly afterwards, when the little party broke up and the two young women made their way back to their lodgings, they were still chuckling at the farmers' reminiscences.

'At least,' Fran remarked to Ada that evening, 'I now know the source of the huge voice that resonates across the moors at times – Gowan Pickering!'

'Was it he, do you think, who was responsible for the comment made by one of your pupils that day you told me about?' queried Ada. 'You remember? One of his children complained that he was beaten for not responding to his father's call and said he simply thought his father had been talking to his dog!'

'I think that's him,' confirmed Fran. 'Mr Gowan Pickering has a powerful voice and a powerful presence. And his children know it!'

The rest of Ada and Fran's holiday was taken up with long walks around the area. On their last night together, they were in a reflective mood. They sat on a mossy knoll, their backs to the rough moor, gazing out to sea where the moon made a silver river across its restlessness, and ships had become ghostly outlines as the light faded.

'Thank you, Fran, for an unforgettable week,' said Ada. 'This is such familiar territory to you, but it's been a glimpse of another world to me and I'll not forget it.' She sighed. She had enjoyed their holiday, yet it had left her with mixed emotions. The contrast between much of the life she saw in Whitby and that of the moorland seemed acute.

She chewed pensively on a blade of grass. 'I find it so difficult,' she murmured, almost to herself, 'to link the pretty water colours I see with the life I've witnessed here. My landlady has a treasured picture of a little girl cradling the body of a tiny bird in her arms, yet here people rejoice at the sight of dozens of grouse dying before their eyes at the shoot. And you've told me yourself that girls as young as six or seven are taught to wring the necks of chickens.

'I see sketches of country workers and their children picnicking in fields abundant with grain whilst here the children's hands are calloused and their arms bruised with heavy labour. I contrast the loving mother and her children in pretty, flower-strewn gardens depicted in pastel shades with the careworn farm women hoeing their vegetable plots whilst their undernourished children collect the produce, not for decoration but for food. And the men depicted in many popular scenes are dashing individuals with well-tailored garments, whilst the farmers on the moors are clad in heavy tweed, solidly constructed boots and caps to protect them from the elements. Their pleasure lies in the thrill of the kill and the power of their muscles over the unforgiving earth. We are the products of a Victorian England, Fran. Our appreciation of the countryside is clouded in sentimentality. Prints of Constable's *Haywain* is a town-person's view of harvest, and Millais' *Ophelia* is a way of dealing with the ugliness of death.'

Fran was taken aback by her friend's thoughts. She had found her venture into country life so invigorating that she was hard pressed to understand Ada's eloquently expressed and emotional outburst. She knew Ada was a sensitive girl, despite her down-to-earth Scottish façade, a girl who loved poetry and literature. Her imagination appealed to the romantic in Fran. Yet, not for the first time, their interpretation of what they had enjoyed together conflicted.

She remonstrated. 'But think of the fun of the hunt, Ada,

and the exhilaration of the shoot. And remember the delights of this beautiful place.'

'Is your enjoyment of the sport of these places and the magnificence of its setting all that influences your attitude, or is there a certain gentleman in your thoughts?' Ada asked.

Fran looked startled. 'Whatever makes you say that?'

'I saw you enjoying the attentions of a certain Mr Gowan Pickering whilst we were at the shoot, and I saw you blush at his greeting to you.' Ada was determined to understand her friend's attitude. 'I think you have developed a deep respect for the people of this land, Fran, but I also think that you have a particular liking for a man. His charisma has drawn you to an empathy with his kind.'

'I'll thank you to keep such thoughts to yourself,' retorted Fran. 'Mr Pickering is a fine man, but he is father to eight children and probably twice my age. I think you are impertinent to imply any impropriety!'

'I'm sorry,' soothed Ada. 'I spoke out of turn. I value our friendship and have no desire to compromise it. This has been a wonderful experience, which I wouldn't have had without you. I ask you to forgive me.'

'I forgive you,' replied Fran, relieved. 'I think the loveliness of this place and the delights of the holiday have affected us both. Let us be friends, Ada, and let us dismiss this silliness.'

SIX

Smiling faces and eager questioning greeted Fran when she reopened her little school after the summer break.

'My father says you were at the hunt. Did you enjoy it?' from one of the Harland boys.

'Did you like the shoot, Miss?' from some of the other pupils.

She smiled, but the parents' appreciation of her involvement with their children's lives changed dramatically later in the school year.

'Bloody government!' from one.

'Who does that Campbell Bannerman think he is?' said another, whose look of disgust emphasised her frustration. 'I thought Prime Ministers were supposed to take care of foreign stuff and not interfere wi' the likes of us. What you going to do about t' new laws, Miss Booth?'

Fran was feeling the backlash from her family's revered Liberal Government's latest attempts to improve the lot of the working population by raising educational standards. On Fylingdales, unwelcome interference from an unpopular Liberal government was having an impact on her day-to-day life and, at times, she was hard-pressed to deal with it.

'I'm not blaming you personally, ma'am, but is it true I can't bring my little Polly to school until she's five?'

'We've got illness in t' family, Miss. Can't you just mek an exception and help us by takin' in t' little uns? T' government'll not find out, will they?'

Fran had to explain that new legislation had to be obeyed,

despite the local families traditionally having sent their children to school at three or, in the case of illness, whenever they thought appropriate, but secretly she was delighted. Life in the schoolroom was a lot easier without the presence of children who were often little more than babies. Five years old, she thought, was perfectly reasonable.

Another piece of legislation that affected her life was easier to deal with: the introduction of free school meals for the needy. Being a Church of England foundation school, the local church representatives on the Education Committee were anxiously considering the logistics of supplying food to the school's remote location. The question became academic, however, when the local populace unanimously rejected the prospect of their children being fed by an outside agency.

If compliance with the law had been less fraught, Fran would have encouraged the parents to seek help regardless of the stigma that they would have faced. Many of her pupils were undernourished, and the ubiquitous bread and dripping or bread and ham fat that they brought to school did not provide a balanced diet. But fate determined that the problem was taken out of her hands.

She tried in vain to explain to her family in Whitby that moorland people were proud, independent and averse to any interference in their lives, but Henry Campbell Bannerman was a hero to the Booth family, and to them this was the beginning of a new era in social care.

The parents who sought her advice about the admission of their children to her little school were decidedly not of the same opinion. Amongst those who visited Howdale School was Gowan Pickering. 'Now then, lass!' he greeted her. 'I suppose our little schoolma'am is happy to ha' t' little 'uns banned from school, eh? Next, tha'll be wanting 'em to stay wi thee 'till they're more n' thirteen!'

He had arrived at the end of the day after the children had left. His manner was, as always, relaxed and confident and he sat on the edge of a desk, his long legs stretching out across the floor and his arms folded. He chuckled and his resonant voice filled the little schoolroom. 'Does't tha' remember being annoyed at my Reg leaving when he were twelve ... well, going on thirteen? We needed him on t' farm but tha' didn't look impressed at that!'

Fran drew herself up to her full height and donned a serious expression. 'I thought the boy had promise,' she replied. 'I hope you're not going to tell me that all your children will do the same. It is disheartening for them to feel encouragement from me but know that their studies are little valued in their homes. And it's even worse when they know they have potential but it will never be realised.'

Gowan Pickering had a habit of assuming that his views were universally accepted, and that his position in society gave him rights over all he surveyed. His response to Fran's brave chastisement was one which, in retrospect, she might have forecast. He laughed.

His voice resonated round the room. 'Our little schoolteacher has a mind of her own, I see! And she concerns herself wi' the welfare of t' children in her care! Yet I will remind her that I make t' decisions regarding my family's best interests. I will choose whether my children will benefit from more time wi' their studies. You and your family might have a very different view to that o' t' moorland folks like me, but I'll strike a bargain wi' you, schoolma'am. You will let me see t' records of my children's achievements – or lack of 'em – and when t' picture is clear, I will tell you if they will be able to benefit from schooling when they turn thirteen.'

Fran was embarrassed. Had she overstepped the mark in suggesting that she had a right to interfere with a father's duty to make decisions in the best interests of his family? She found herself apologising. 'I am sorry, sir. My own father is most diligent in decision making regarding his family, and I do not expect any less of you. I will, of course, supply you with information about your children's work, but I leave the final decision about their futures in your capable hands. I will begin now.'

She felt flustered, but she opened her records and showed them to Gowan. 'Look. Elizabeth has achieved high grades in all her subjects and she's a pleasure to teach. Ethel is conscientious and neat in her work.'

Gowan beamed with pleasure. 'But what about t' lads?' he asked.

'Alfred is struggling,' Fran replied. 'He wants nothing more than to be amongst the animals. He has no liking for school, or ability in his subjects. But young Gowan is a clever boy and is doing work well in advance of his age. I feel sure he could have a promising future and probably enter the grammar school.'

'So, when it comes to schoolwork, it will be with Elizabeth and Gowan that my hopes for t' future rest,' Gowan said. 'I will make sure I keep a watchful eye on them, Miss Booth. To that end, I think I will return to your schoolroom very soon. My mother has remarked that you and your family ha' a very different view o' t' role of girls but t' Pickerings are not insensitive to t' help given by good people like yourself. For now, I will bid thee good day, lass, and simply say thank you.'

Fran watched Gowan Hodgson Pickering mount the horse, which he had tethered outside the entrance to the school, and ride away along the track that climbed towards Thorney Brow farm. His figure on horseback was erect; he was relaxed and at one with the animal.

As she returned to the schoolroom to put away the paperwork she had shown him, she could feel a difference in the room. His presence had filled it and now it felt empty. His voice had resonated and now there was silence. She found herself looking forward to his next visit. She justified her anticipation by reasoning that it was good to meet a man who was prepared to take time out of his day to enquire about his children's welfare. So few parents did the same.

Yet, as she tidied away not only the documents she had shown Gowan but also the remnants of the day's work, she remembered her conversation with Ada and blushed. Did she find him attractive? He was tall and seemed to tower over her diminutive and slender frame. He was muscular, some would say athletic. She conjured up a picture of his face. He had well-defined features, a firm jaw, dark-brown eyes not unlike her own, and a fine moustache. His countenance was marked by exposure to the elements, but he had laughter lines around the eyes. 'Yes,' she concluded. 'He is an attractive man.'

She emptied a pail of water onto the earth outside the door and replaced its contents from the beck that ran at the back of the building. Back in the schoolroom, as she cleaned the tables stained by the children's attempts to paint plants, leaves and fungi, her mind dwelt on Gowan's character. Had she found that attractive, too? She was not sure. She knew that the charismatic, sociable elements of his nature were appealing and much admired by others who saw him as one who never accepted defeat. He was a powerful advocate for country life and his lead was followed unquestioningly. Yet she detected a selfishness, possibly a wilfulness in him and, judging by his enthusiasm for hunting and shooting which she had witnessed, a recklessness and a relish of the cruel acts of killing that she found disconcerting.

'I think there is more to Mr Pickering's character than a casual observer would observe,' she decided.

As she carefully prepared a set of slates and chalks for the next day, she concluded that her mind was far too concerned with analysing a man who was, after all, no more than a concerned parent. 'I think I can attribute my silly musings to Ada,' she decided. 'She is a lovely friend but should, perhaps, be more inclined to keep her thoughts to herself and refrain from filling my head with nonsense.'

The following weeks saw Gowan Pickering become a regular visitor to the little school on the moor. Fran knew that Elizabeth Estill, Ethel Jane, Gowan and Alfred Harold were being singled out, for there were seven other Pickering children in her care. Five of them were William and Mary's children: Mary, Henry, George, Alice and Walter. There were also John and Rebecca, the son and daughter of John Pickering and his frail wife, Rebecca. No other Pickering, or representatives of such large families as the Harlands, Stubbs or Collinsons, visited the school or enquired after their offsprings' well-being.

On each of his visits, Fran showed Gowan her carefully kept records. When Elizabeth's work was consistently above average, she delighted in his obvious pride in his daughter. He mentioned the possibility of her attending school in Whitby when she was older and said he had spoken to her about her work. Elizabeth had said that she would like to be a teacher when she grew up, and Gowan and Fran laughed at the compliment she had inadvertently paid her own teacher. Gowan remarked that it was no less than Fran deserved, which made her blush with embarrassment and Gowan tease her for her sensitivity.

Increasingly, Gowan's visits became a highlight of her week. She looked forward to their conversations and was discovering his lively sense of humour, which ensured that his presence always meant the promise of laughter. To Fran, having fun was as important in life as having good health. Being one of five girls who had laughed, shared confidences and felt the camaraderie of common experience, this was the thing she had missed most when she took up her isolated position at Howdale School.

September saw the change of seasons as summer greens

turned to autumn golds. The vivid red of the poppies in the hedgerows was replaced with the downy white softness of thistle seeds, and the first fruits of the new season appeared: hazel nuts, blackberries and, high on the moors, bilberries.

Fran looked forward to the October half-term holiday and the prospect of being spoilt by her mother and father, welcomed by her sisters and taking advantage of Whitby's shops, markets, tea shops and restaurants, but she still revelled in the beauty of the moors and cliffs of Fylingdales.

On the eve of her departure, she stood on a high point looking out to sea and soaked in the beauty of the scene as the setting sun left silvery ripples on the water. So deep was her reverie that it startled her when a familiar voice broke the magic.

Gowan Pickering had dismounted from his horse a little way up the track and stolen up on her. She greeted him with a timorous, 'Good afternoon, sir.'

He responded with his usual laugh. 'I caught thee unawares, lass,' he said. 'I have no wish to disturb this tranquil scene, but I thought to catch you before you leave for Whitby. When will you go?'

'Not until tomorrow,' she explained. 'It'll be too late for a train tonight. May I ask why you enquire?'

'Tha' may. All I can say is that I've enjoyed our time together talking about my children, and I thought to recompense thee for t' hours I've tek'n from tha' day. Would tha' agree to accompany me on a visit to Falling Foss? I think I remember you remarking that tha'd not seen t' waterfall and I think you would like it. Will tha' come?'

Fran was taken aback. She felt a surge of mixed emotions: excitement, surprise, uncertainty, pleasure, trepidation. She found it difficult to reply and stuttered, 'My parents are expecting me. I think I cannot let them down.'

'Why not go to Whitby tomorrow but return a little earlier

than tha'd planned? Tha' has a holiday and, if we want to see t' foss, we'd be better to go before t' winter arrives,' he argued.

'I would like that,' she replied uncertainly. 'I admit I have longed to visit the foss, but I'm not sure.'

'Why?' he questioned.

'Your suggestion is a surprise. I didn't expect it.'

There was a note of teasing sarcasm in his voice as he responded. 'So our little schoolma'am dislikes surprises. I thought I knew you better. Is your life so regimented that ye canna' put aside a time for enjoyment? I have constant demands on my time, yet I relish a chance to enjoy myself and I think you would enjoy t' foss.'

Fran hesitated briefly, but then she agreed. 'Yes,' she said, 'I think I would like that very much.'

'Then, 'tis settled. I will collect tha' from tha' lodgings next Saturday at nine in t' morning and we will visit Falling Foss. I look forward to it. Meanwhile, I wish you a good day.' Gowan mounted his horse and, without a glance behind him, rode away.

Fran watched him disappear around the bend in the track and suddenly felt slightly faint. What had she done? She had agreed to go to a place she longed to see, but which she should not visit with a man and no chaperone. What would she tell her parents? What had possessed her? What would her landlady think? What would happen when the children in her care heard of her adventure? News travelled quickly on the moors, and children were the greatest source of information about the activities of their elders.

But she had given her word and made a promise. The deed was as good as done. She returned to the schoolroom, collected her books, locked the school door and returned to her lodgings to request that she might return early from her half-term break.

That night, she slept badly.

SEVEN

FRAN HAD BEEN looking forward to the half-term holiday. She returned to Whitby as she had planned but, unusually, became reticent when her sisters asked about her plans and for up-to-date news of her life on Howdale Moor. She felt guilty when she told a little lie and said that she had a lot of preparation to do for the coming term and had to return early.

She lay in bed one night and longed for sleep to lull her restless mind. The sounds of life around her had become an irritant; no longer were the noises of harbour life a comfort, and she blamed them for her insomnia. No longer was 14 St Ann's Staith a place of sanctuary; it was where she was expected to account for herself. No longer was home a place of refuge; it was where she now felt a misfit. Yet, in her heart of hearts, she knew that the cause of her discontent lay in her own actions. 'I am no better than the strumpets who frequent the taverns of the town,' she decided.

Friday came. Fran took leave of her family and returned to the moors. On Saturday, true to his word, Gowan arrived with the farm cart, helped her climb aboard and whipped the horse to a trot. They set off along the track that skirted Howdale Farm where he slowed the horse to a walk to negotiate an incline, and then increased its pace as they passed Cook House. The ground levelled, and they joined the Scarborough Road where the road was paved and the cart moved more easily.

To their left, rough ground was interspersed with fast-flowing becks and tiny, sparkling waterfalls. To their right, dry-stone walls divided pasture land into fields where cows, sheep and horses grazed. Their rough coats betrayed their pedigree, for only the sturdiest of animals could survive exposure to the harsh elements and terrain of the moorland farms.

The sun appeared from behind wispy clouds, and the landscape was illuminated. Grasses sparkled with jewels of moisture, and the roof of the Flask Inn to their left was covered in a steamy mist as the night's rain dried in the morning warmth.

The tension that Fran had felt when she joined Gowan that morning eased. They barely spoke until they were past Pond Farm, other than to remark on the weather and for him to enquire whether she was comfortable. Now it seemed as if the day had properly begun.

He asked teasingly, 'Well, little schoolma'am, does t' transport in a farmer's cart suit thee?'

She laughed. 'It suits me well, sir, and I'm delighted with the perspective my vantage point gives me. I feel so much more a part of the landscape than I ever do on my journeys by train, and I love the clean, fresh air brushing my face.'

Gowan looked delighted. 'I thought t'would suit you,' he chuckled.

They left the road near Kirk Moor Beck where its rushing water bubbled through a culvert. Low Moor stretched away on either side, and Gowan pointed out areas of bog where he had seen horsemen struggle to extricate themselves when they had taken an ill-advised route when hunting. He laughed when he recounted the story of a rider who had shouted for help. The other huntsmen simply advised each other to rescue the saddle and bridle, giving the hapless huntsman the impression they were going to leave him to fend for himself because they valued his equipment more than him or his horse.

Gowan's humour and the delightful warmth of the sun meant that Fran was feeling content as the horse and cart entered the wooded area that led to Falling Foss. She delighted in seeing trees that couldn't survive on the exposed acres of moorland but thrived here. Rough hawthorn was hardly noticeable as its berries competed for attention with the marble-like reds and whites of snowberries. These were interspersed with alder, encouraged in its growth by the moist soil, whilst ivy, columbine and honeysuckle competed for survival.

As the track dropped more steeply, outcrops of grey, slate-like boulders broke through the undergrowth, and she could hear trickling water negotiating the undulating ground. The woodland grew denser and darker. Shafts of light illuminated glades and the brown and silver bark of birch, the red, gold and yellow sycamore leaves, and the glowing mountain ash berries.

Fran was entranced, and she almost wished that she need go no further. Although Falling Foss was their destination, the spectacle that she was witnessing was enough to justify their journey. Her voice was barely audible as she murmured, 'I did not dream of seeing such beauty. Thank you, sir.'

Gowan looked delighted. He had intended to take her to a place that was very special but, despite his joviality, he had not been insensitive to her apprehension when he had suggested the outing. Now he had been exonerated; he had done what he intended to do and introduced her to an experience she might not have had otherwise. And the best was still to come.

In response, he simply said, 'I thought tha'd like it, lass. And how about a bit less of the "sir"? Tha' knows my name is Gowan. I will call you by the name thy friends use. I like "Fran". 'Tis a good name.'

Fran made no response. As she gazed about her, relishing the view, she became aware of a thundering sound that was getting louder. They were almost at the Foss. Gowan told her that he would release his horse from the shafts of the cart and leave it to graze on a grassy verge. The rest of their journey must be done on foot. He offered his hand to help her to the ground, attended to his horse and cart, and they set off along a narrow, winding path.

The sight of Falling Foss came as a surprise to Fran, despite the warning sounds that preceded their arrival. The view was obscured by a turn in the track, a camouflage of greenery and a proliferation of rocks and boulders until suddenly it appeared in front of them. The waterfall was in full spate, dropping into a steep, dark ravine, and the sight of it took her breath away. The noise, the spray that threatened to soak onlookers if they came too near, the height of the cliff from which the water crashed onto the rocks below, the flicker of delicate rainbows above the spectacle where shafts of sunlight met moist air, the vivid green of bracken, lichen and moss, all assaulted her senses. She gasped with delight.

First she stood rigidly, absorbing the view, then she stepped forward as if to be a part of it, to feel the spray on her face. A firm arm reached out and held her.

'Not too close, Fran,' Gowan said. 'T' ground's slippery. I don't want tha' in t' ravine.'

His voice, the warmth of his body and his breath next to her face broke the spell, but not for long. She stood with his arms around her, the restless water contrasting with the feeling of security that engulfed her and their silence an antidote to the noise of the torrent.

Gowan relaxed his hold, and they were able to pick out tiny details that combined to create the scene. He pointed to a willow sapling whose tender roots could scarcely cling to the steep sides of the embankment that flanked the ravine. They saw a solitary robin perched high on a branch, and a squirrel darting up the trunk of a tree to shake the moisture off its fur when it reached its hiding place. Fran spotted tiny anemones struggling for survival in dry cracks and crevices, and speedwell covering the gaps in the roots of a tall birch.

They absorbed the sight, and words became unnecessary as they silently acknowledged their shared pleasure. They both accepted that the other's company enhanced the experience. No words were needed when they moved further along the path. Here, as the sound of water lessened, they watched the light change as the landscape became less dramatic.

The silence was only broken when they reached the Hermitage. 'Look,' Gowan said and pointed at an enormous boulder out of which a folly had been carved and the word 'Hermitage' engraved into it. It was an extraordinary sight, big enough to allow a person to enter the cavernous hole hewn from its centre and with a flat top on which a visitor might sit. He laughed at her incredulity.

'Why would anyone go to such lengths to create something so silly and yet so appealing?' Fran joined in his laughter as she ran to the extraordinary structure, unable to resist the temptation to touch it, peer inside it and, to his amusement, climb on its top. She waved to him as he stood on the path below. He teased her that he would not help if she got stuck, and that he would walk away and leave her there. Then he reached up and lifted her down and she giggled as her skirt caught the draught and billowed out behind her.

'I love to see you laugh, little schoolma'am,' he remarked, and hugged her.

It was a spontaneous gesture, kind and loving, and she responded. She felt freer than she had ever felt. There were no relatives to dictate protocol, no children to demand that a standard of behaviour be observed, no rules to determine correct action or speech. She was happy.

Gowan suggested it was time to eat. The day had been exciting but tiring, and Fran had to admit that food and something to quench her thirst would be appreciated. He guided her further along the path as it wound its way through the woodland to Midge Hall. This small stone cottage had a reputation for serving basic but well-cooked food to visitors.

They sat in a tiny room at a table covered with a white cloth, and were offered apple pie with a slice of cheese and a pot of tea. They were warm after their walk but began to feel a chill in the air and, as soon as Gowan had paid the proprietor and complimented her on the fine spread, they left and returned to his horse.

Walking back, he held Fran's hand as he guided her past rough stones that littered the path and round muddy patches of earth. It seemed so natural that she barely noticed. When they reached the place where his horse was tethered, she watched as he took the horse to a stream to let it drink and then reattached the shafts of the cart to its harness. He helped her climb aboard and they set off on the return journey, anxious to avoid travelling in the dusk but relaxed and comfortable in each other's presence.

They talked of the day they had enjoyed and the beauty of the moors as the light faded. Gowan reminisced about the heatwave of the preceding August, when harvesting had been particularly testing and the animals had needed constant attention as the becks dried up and there were unusual water shortages. Fran delighted in the confidences he shared with her. She laughed at the antics of his infant children, sympathised over his sister's inability to leave home despite her impending marriage, and shared his sadness that his family was dispersed.

When they arrived at Brow, Gowan helped her down from the cart. She thanked him for such an enjoyable day and he suggested they meet again.

Sunday was traditionally the day when church attendance was expected, work on the farm was reduced to a minimum, and saddles were soaped, bridles cleaned, and guns primed in readiness for the next shoot. He saw no reason why they should not take a walk together if the weather was fine. She agreed, and unlike the occasion of his first invitation, this time she did not hesitate. Gone were the scruples that had caused her sleepless nights and gone was the uncertainty of bucking social mores. She had felt the warmth of a man's companionship and experienced the joy of shared pleasure. For the first time in her life she felt responsible for her own destiny, and the prospect of another day of Gowan's company was a welcome one.

When the next day dawned cold but bright and dry, the couple made their way to a point at Stoupe Beck where the rough moorland scrub and pasture land ended and rocky cliffs tumbled down to the sea. The tide was out, and they walked on damp, golden sand.

Gowan held Fran's hand; they laughed, and he told her she was beautiful. She flirted with him, releasing her dark hair from its usual carefully tied bun and tossing her head to allow it to fall in a way that she knew was attractive. She allowed him to help her to her feet after they had sat for a while to look at the sea and taste the salty air. He put his arm around her as a chill wind reminded them that this was autumn and she shivered despite warm clothing.

They identified their several differences: her upbringing in the town and his in the countryside; her affection for books and lively imagination, and his more pragmatic approach to the vicissitudes of life.

He increased his hold on her as they sat with their backs to the rocks. She felt his arms tighten around her shoulders and then his lips pressed against hers. She had never experienced a man's kiss before and was startled. She drew back from his hold, unsure of her response, but he laughed and pressed his lips more firmly against hers. She felt the coarseness of his face against hers, his calloused hands rough against her clothing and the muscles of his body strain against hers. Momentarily, she was afraid and wanted to run away, but then her body became limp.

She felt a change in him; there was a tenderness now as he stroked her hair, caressed her, and whispered her name. The effect on her was profound; it was as if she had begun a new existence. She felt a warm surge rush throughout her body, and an odd tremor deep inside her that she had never experienced before, but which was strangely pleasurable. She responded, allowing his tongue to explore her mouth and his hands to caress her body. She touched the back of his head, his face, his neck, and wound her fingers through his hair.

Suddenly, he let her go. 'You have quite an influence on me, little schoolma'am!' he chuckled.

Fran was silent, embarrassed. She pushed back her tousled hair and readjusted her skirt. She looked down at the ground, ashamed of her own behaviour but knowing that her effect on him was equally strong. Being kissed by a man had produced a strange mixture of fear, excitement, tension and a joyous release from moral constraint. But this was not just any man, it was a man to whom she was attracted and of whom she had become fond. Now she knew the feeling was mutual.

As the light faded, they made their way back to her lodgings. There seemed no need for conversation. As she turned to walk through the Petty family's allotment, Gowan said he would call on her during the week and she said that she would like that very much.

Alice Petty greeted her lodger with a knowing smile and offered her supper. Having eaten a little and exchanged pleasantries, Fran retired to bed that night with her head reeling with unresolved questions. Obviously her landlady knew of her liaison with Gowan, but what would her family think if they knew of her exploits? They would be horrified!

Gowan was so different to the men in Whitby where the

chapel, the Mission to Seamen and families of tailors, dress-makers or milliners were their friends. He was so different to her gentle, softly spoken father. The novels she read had depicted worthy men as being polite and considerate, yet Gowan had a magnetism that she found impossible to resist and a rough-ness that was both frightening and comforting because of its strength.

She decided that her affair would be a secret. She would not speak of it, and she would allow the passage of time to deter-mine the outcome of this new experience. She was flattered, ex-cited, apprehensive and overwhelmed, but this man enchanted her. She was spellbound by the hint of danger that she felt in his presence and attracted by the raw emotion he exuded.

EIGHT

IT WAS CHRISTMAS and Sarah was feeling especially pleased with herself. She had achieved her ambition: she and John were now the proud owners of 50 Flowergate, Whitby.

'I think I'll try and make this a very special evening, dear,' she remarked to her husband as she donned her coat and prepared for a trip to the market. 'We've been so lucky this year. A lovely new home, a Christmas to remember, and good prospects for the new year. Fran's leaving tomorrow and we might not see her again until the spring, poor girl. Do you remember last year? Snow, blizzards! It might have been wet this year, but at least she's been able to join us for the festive season.'

John smiled. 'You've done a good job, Sarah. This is indeed a fine new home, but it's you who makes it so! Our girls are lucky to have a mother like you. And you're right, 1908 looks promising. Why, we might even see an improvement in Rose's handiwork!' He chuckled and Sarah couldn't resist laughing with him.

'That girl'll be the death of us, John, but at least we've been able to put a roof over her head when she couldn't pay her rent. Will she ever learn?'

Outside, Sarah pulled her shawl tightly round her and headed to the Staith then over the bridge into the hubbub of the market. This was the Whitby that she loved – all human life represented, all human needs satisfied. The densely clustered area gave her a feeling of security, of belonging, of familiarity. She shuddered as she thought of one of her daughters leaving this spot for her lonely life on the moors, and of the problems that isolation could bring, especially at times of illness.

'Surely,' she thought, 'a convivial meal and the company of her family will do the trick this year. Fran must have had enough adventure by now. And she could easily get a job in one of the Whitby schools.'

Sarah headed straight for a trader she had dealt with many times before. Tucked on one side of the busy market, Mr Armitage sold medicines and remedies, and she needed his expertise for Mary. Poor Mary had suffered chesty coughs all her life, and for the last few days the girl had been wheezing and coughing. Sarah was annoyed with herself, for she had run out of medicine at precisely the time when she knew it was most needed. She considered the words of a neighbour who, when she heard of the Booth family's move to Flowergate, had remarked, 'All that heat and all that gas in t' air'll na' help yon lass's chest.'

Mr Armitage was a stout man with a florid complexion and a bushy greying beard. He tugged his forelock politely. 'Good morning, Mrs Booth. I hope you and the family are well.'

Sarah was pleased. Her new home gave her status in the town, and she enjoyed the rather fawning respect that the tradesmen gave her. Mr Armitage knew Sarah well and had no hesitation in finding the usual kaolin poultice and cough mixture for Mary.

Next she made her way to Mr Purvis's grocery in Church Street. Just as she arrived, a young boy scampered away from the shop, hotly pursued by Mr Purvis. Hot and flustered, the shop owner greeted her. 'Ah, Mrs Booth! How lovely to see you. I'm so sorry if I frightened you, but that young lad was stealing tobacco and I wanted to catch him.'

'Oh dear! You poor man! Did he manage to take the tobacco?' Sarah looked concerned.

'Sadly, he did,' Mr Purvis answered. 'He wanted to buy it but the new legislation stops me selling alcohol or tobacco to children. The boy has been smoking for years and only wanted a small plug. I'm afraid I cannot support this government's interference in such matters, Mrs Booth. I only sell the best leaves and they're clean. I really can't see what harm they're doing!'

Sarah nodded her agreement. 'This government has good intentions, Mr Purvis, but they've got little understanding of the liking for tobacco amongst the young. I admit I sympathise with you for doubtless that lad's not the only one to be affected. And you're right – I shop with you, so I can vouch for the quality of what you sell.'

Having placed her order and received a promise that an errand boy would deliver before nightfall, Sarah made her way home in a buoyant mood, full of stories about her trip. She was looking forward to a lovely evening with her family.

'Poor Mr Purvis,' she remarked to Hannah and Lily. 'We really need to support our government. Dear Mr Asquith has tried so hard to help the poor, but he seems to have caused Mr Purvis some problems. Would you believe it? Young lads can no longer buy tobacco and they're stealing it.'

But Hannah was obviously not listening. She and Lily gave each other knowing looks and Sarah decided it was one of those moments when she'd interrupted her girls sharing secrets. Years of living with them had taught her that it was sometimes better not to enquire. 'They'll doubtless tell me when they want to,' she thought. 'No point in making a mountain out of a molehill.'

But Sarah was puzzled. They seldom hid their criticism of Rose because Rose was – well, just Rose! Sarah had lost count of the number of times the girl had left home to start a new life, the number of times she had brought home her latest protégé only to find that her heart had ruled her head and he or she was a lost cause; the number of times clients who had accepted her offer to alter or replace their dresses had complained about the quality of her work and long-suffering Hannah had been brought in to save the family's reputation. The conspiratorial glances between Hannah and Lily could result from a conversation about Rose, but she doubted it.

The meal that evening was good, and afterwards in the parlour John poured each of them a glass of Burgundy whilst Lily sat at the piano and accompanied them as they sang 'I'm a Yankee Doodle Dandy' and 'Give My Regards to Broadway'. They laughed as Rose tried her hand at 'The Entertainer'; much to their amusement, she decided that Scott Joplin was a fine composer whose work even she could master.

The atmosphere was convivial. Sarah was satisfied that she and John could be proud of their daughters and that 1908 would be a year that they could look forward to with equanimity.

It was when Lily struck up the chords of 'I Can't Tell Why I Love You But I Do' that Sarah's feeling of well-being was shattered. Hannah whispered to her sister, 'This is for you,' and Sarah noticed Fran blush and glance uncomfortably in her direction.

Rose, not to be outdone, remarked, 'This one's for me, Lily.'

Hannah's look of horror accompanied her immediate response. 'What on earth do you mean, Rose?'

That elicited a grin from Rose and a quick reply, 'Lily's playing for George and me.'

'George who?' exclaimed Hannah, her look of consternation very obvious.

'George Easton, of course,' replied Rose.

'You mean the Eastons of Church Street? Those ne'er-do-wells with all those children! The ones whose father pretends to be a joiner-carpenter but who couldn't fix a broken piece of furniture if his life depended on it? And whose son George drinks enough for a regiment of soldiers?' retorted an angry Hannah.

'You are so rude and so lacking in understanding.' It was

Rose's turn to be annoyed. 'George is a lovely man, and I've walked out with him twice. He is very gentlemanly.'

Fran looked concerned. 'Oh, do think twice, Rose! He's really not suitable for you.'

Hannah's face changed to one of disgust. Turning to Fran, she quipped, 'Well, you're a fine one to talk!'

Fran blushed and fell silent. The atmosphere in the room, only minutes before relaxed and convivial, felt charged with emotion.

Sarah looked to John for support, but he remained silent, as was his wont. She felt disinclined to discover the truth behind Hannah's remark to Fran, or to give Rose the opportunity to expand on what was, presumably, her latest project. Yet the evening was no longer a delightful end to the season of goodwill, and suddenly she had forebodings about the forthcoming year. She decided to suggest that Lily play a more appropriate piece on the piano and vowed to pursue her enquiries the next day.

The evening ended with a spirited rendition of Elgar's 'Pomp and Circumstance' and a gentler 'Abide With Me'. As they retired to bed, Sarah planned her conversation with two of her daughters before Fran left for the wild moorlands and Rose became too entangled with a young man for whom Sarah had little regard.

The next day dawned and heavy flakes of snow suggested the type of weather that always left Sarah worried about Fran's work on Fylingdales. The girl had said she was leaving that day as she had preparation to do for her pupils, but Sarah had noticed that 'preparation' figured in her reasons for returning to the moors with increasing frequency. She now wondered if there was a different reason for her daughter's eagerness to start work.

She was about to broach the subject as she and Fran cleared away the breakfast dishes when Rose interrupted with an announcement that she was off to see one of the Pearsons in Harkers' Buildings. These tenements were overcrowded, lacked sanitation and were a breeding ground for disease. Rose seldom visited such places without bringing home head lice or fleas; Sarah hated the thought of having to get out her nit comb for Rose's benefit, but she knew her protests would be futile. The prospect of spending hours carefully combing Rose's hair over a piece of paper to extract the lice, and of treating her again for the effects of flea bites, was becoming a regular event, but not one Sarah relished. But she felt she could not complain, for the family Rose referred to were distant relatives of hers, and Mary Pearson was about to give birth to her seventh child. Five of her previous pregnancies had produced babies that had died within their first year of life, and Rose was firmly convinced that the reason for the deaths was that the babies had been boys. Sarah agreed. She had lost four babies and, much to John's distress, they were all boys. Sarah, Fran and Rose knew that childbirth was a terrible time for women, but to give birth to a boy was to compound the problems of rearing fragile new life.

Rose left on her mission and Sarah took the opportunity to talk about childbirth as her starting point for a conversation which she hoped would shed some light on Fran's secret. She was convinced that her daughter was harbouring a secret that was almost certainly concerned with a member of the opposite sex.

'Poor Mary Pearson,' she remarked. 'Childbirth is a blessing and a curse. I have five beautiful daughters, but so many lives are lost, so many women scarred for life and so many babies born to die. Any woman who marries must know that the man she weds will give her babies. She must only marry when she knows that man can provide not only for her but for the family they will have. Tell me, dear, am I right in thinking you have met a man? Is this the secret you have shared with Hannah and Lily?

Don't blame them. They've not betrayed your confidence, but I worry about you and I want to know that, if you should find someone to share your life, he will care for you. I am only acting as a concerned mother should. Can you confide in me?'

Fran looked taken aback. Part of her now regretted confiding in her sisters, though another part of her was glad because she was not a secretive person. She hesitated, and that alone was enough to prove to Sarah that her daughter had something to hide.

Her mother's look of distress was enough to convince Fran that an explanation was needed. 'I will confide in you, Mother,' she began. 'But you must promise to hear me out and not prejudge the man I speak of.'

Sarah nodded her agreement.

Fran told her mother about Gowan Pickering. She told of his standing in the community as a respected farmer and huntsman; of his love for his children; of the tragic death of his first wife; of his support for his mother and his delightful relationship with his brother, William. She spoke of his reputation as hard-working, trustworthy and valued member of the Fylingdales community, and of his good looks, commanding presence and, above all, of his affection for her. Her eyes glowed and her face became animated. She was sure that such a eulogy would elicit a favourable reaction. She quivered in anticipation as she waited for a response. None came.

Sounds from the street outside, muffled by the heavy curtains in the room, seemed louder. George, the grandfather clock in the hall, ticked his solid, regular beat. One of the lodgers called to ask if there was anyone in the kitchen, but they made no attempt to answer him. At last, as if recovering from a near mortal blow, Sarah took a deep breath and spoke, her voice tense but quiet, her body rigid. 'Is this the man who lost his wife in childbirth some years ago? I remember you being very upset.'

'Yes.'

'How old is he?'

'Forty-one.'

'How many children does he have?'

'Eight.'

'And where do they live?'

'With relatives, although some of the youngest live with his mother and sister at the big house, Thorney Brow.'

'And where does Mr Pickering live?'

'At Browside Cottage with his oldest two, Reginald and John Clark.'

'And does Mr Pickering intend to reunite himself with his children one day?'

'Yes.'

Sarah looked at her daughter's face. The tell-tale signs of discomfort told her that Fran knew she was unlikely to gain parental support, and more words seemed unnecessary. Yet Sarah steeled herself and explained in measured, firm tones as one would to a child the reasons why she was unhappy.

'Thank you, dear, for being so frank with me, but I must ensure that you understand why I am unhappy with what you tell me. This can be no more than infatuation. You are twenty-seven, this man is over forty. He lives on the wild Fylingdale Moor, where the people are little more than heathens. He epitomises all that we deplore. He has an attachment to the Anglican Church. He drinks. He hunts. He will not understand the likes of us, just as we do not understand him. Why, only yesterday I watched men of his type at the inn over the Esk in Whitby and I loathed what I saw. Please, Fran, think again before you consider attaching yourself to a man like this. Leave your job and come back to Whitby – schoolteachers are needed here. Abandon this romantic vision. There are many men here who would be proud to call you their wife.'

Fran's heart sank. She had known that she would face opposition, but to have it articulated so clearly left her feeling misunderstood, alone and angry. 'I see you are more concerned for my welfare when I have an honourable relationship with a respected farmer than you are with Rose, who appears to be walking out with a worthless drunkard. Have you no pride, Mother? Would you incarcerate me here rather than see me happy, whilst you do little to oppose Rose, whose judgement has always been questionable? Do you have double standards for your daughters? Do you favour the one who has always caused you trouble but withdraw support for the one in whom you have taken pride? I am a grown woman and I can make my own decisions. I would like to have your blessing, but I see you do not intend to offer it. I love you and Father, but I will lead my life as I see fit, for I cannot see the harm I do.'

Sarah left the room. A heated argument would not achieve a good result. Having said her piece, she decided that her best course of action was to leave Fran to think about what she had said. She prepared the family's lunch with shaking hands whilst Fran sat on her bed upstairs, wrapped a blanket round her shoulders and wept. That afternoon, she caught her train back to Fylingdales.

NINE

Heavy cloud obscured the horizon and a brisk wind stirred the tops of the hawthorn bushes, making the snow on their branches shed its feathery dust across the path that led to the schoolhouse. Fran waved goodbye to Walter as he trudged away from the building, clutching a book under his arm and pulling his jacket tight across his chest to ward off the chill. She remembered his arrival at the school. He was one of William and Mary Pickering's children and a dull, unimaginative boy about whom the other children cheerfully announced, 'He's not quite right in t' 'ead, Miss.'

'Poor Walter,' she murmured as she closed the schoolhouse door and started clearing away the detritus of the last day of term's work. It was now the Easter holiday and, for her, a momentous occasion.

In the silence of the empty schoolroom, as she raked the ashes from the stove, swept the floor and stacked away the chalks, pencils, books and papers and neatened rows of chairs and desks, she considered her terrible predicament. For some weeks Fran had suspected, then was almost certain, and now she knew. She was pregnant.

She had denied it, tried to wish it were otherwise, but it was true. She shivered. She felt alone. She had not told Gowan because they had argued. He had accused her parents of being typical townsfolk – smug, superior and lacking understanding of the likes of him and his family. She had tried to defend them and she had not seen him for weeks.

She had not told her parents. Somehow she had to inform the world of her condition, to find a place for herself and her unborn child – a bastard, an illegitimate child, an outcast. Somehow she had to face the ignominy and the terror.

She thought of little Walter. Despite his academic inadequacies, he had a home to return to, a family to support him and a recognised place in society. Where would she find a place that would accept a mother with a bastard infant, or where a little lie such as the suggestion that the child's father was dead would be accepted?

She had considered alternatives. Perhaps she could be a governess, move to the city where anonymity would cloak her deceit? She had some savings; perhaps they would be sufficient to provide her with accommodation until after the birth. The thoughts of the birth itself terrified her and she could barely contemplate facing such an ordeal alone. Her head reeled, her self-confidence replaced by a horrible feeling of inadequacy and her decisiveness by dithering uncertainty.

Fran needed a friend. She had written to Ada, and they had arranged to meet in Scarborough as soon as the Easter holiday began. They liked a particular tea shop in the town and on the appointed day, Fran headed there. The tiny shop was adorned with chintz and prided itself on offering quality teas, sandwiches and scones served on delicate china.

Fran was tired and nervous. She chose an inconspicuous table at the side of the room, ordered a pot of tea, and told her hostess that a friend would join her shortly. Then she removed her shawl and gloves and waited.

A brisk wind buffeted the few individuals who had taken to the streets of Scarborough. Summer crowds were still a far-off dream; despite the school holiday being late this year, the weather had not inspired families to venture to the seaside.

Fran sipped her tea and looked through the tiny panes of

glass in the windows of the Georgian-fronted tea room. The youngsters in her classroom had ensured that she maintained at least an outward semblance of calm, and providing meaningful employment for young hands and minds had kept her own mind occupied. But now tears welled up in her eyes and the horrible nausea that had plagued her life recently returned as she sat alone, afraid, helpless.

When Ada finally arrived, full of excitement about a tree that had blown down in the night and blocked a road, preventing the station master from performing his duties and causing havoc to all and sundry, she was greeted by a tearful, white-faced Fran. She was horrified. The lovely reunion she had envisaged was not to be; gossip, laughter, and political discussion were a fantasy.

She took her friend in her arms, indicated to the lady in charge of the establishment that they would like another cup for tea but also a moment of privacy, and gently but firmly demanded an explanation.

Fran was silent, and Ada waited patiently. The tea-shop proprietress eyed the two of them suspiciously but, Ada thought, with compassion, for it was obvious that her friend was in distress.

Fran tried to compose herself, but her voice quivered. 'Oh Ada, it's so lovely to see you. How are you? You must tell me about your work. This weather has been dreadful, hasn't it? It must have a terrible effect on holiday places like this.'

Ada made no comment.

Fran fiddled with her serviette. 'I thought this little cafe might be closed. I'm so glad it's open,' she continued.

Ada interrupted, her face full of concern and kindness. 'Fran, dear. Stop. You don't need to do this. You're not yourself. There's something wrong, isn't there? Do tell me. I'm here for you, my friend.'

At last, quietly in resigned tones and with her eyes downcast, Fran told Ada about her liaison with Gowan Pickering and described her mother's reaction. Finally, she said, 'Ada, I'm pregnant!'

Alone, even until that very morning, she had wondered if she could be mistaken, but now she had confirmed it as a fact. When she had finished her story, she wept freely, but for the first time she felt that a weight had been lifted from her shoulders. She did what she never thought she would be able to do and looked Ada in the eye. Her shame stayed with her, but sharing it had created a bond between them and now she had nothing to hide. She only needed to know Ada's reaction.

When it came, it surprised her. 'Well, the first thing we must do is make sure you get a decent meal inside you,' said Ada. 'You're eating for two now!' And without consultation, she ordered ham, eggs, bread and a fresh pot of tea.

While they waited, she continued, her voice clear and determined. 'You really have been very stupid, Fran, but there's no use crying over spilt milk. We have to decide what you are to do. You don't need me to tell you that you're not the first person in the world to face this dilemma, but you're the first person I've met who has got themselves in quite such a pickle over it. Falling out with your family is one thing, but falling out with the father of your baby is quite another. Most girls in your position would have gone to their lover, told him their plight and forced him to make an honest woman of them. Why do you think you are so different? You must marry this man, Fran. And let me tell you, there are a lot of women who would envy you for he's a good catch. He's got land, status, a reputation as a hard-working farmer, and a following of like-minded country folk who hold him in high esteem. Stop this stupidity, Fran. Tell him. And tell your family too. They have a right to know.'

Fran listened to Ada's outburst in stunned silence. It all

sounded so easy; in Ada's view, it was simply a matter of telling Gowan to marry her. She took a deep breath and was about to reply, but the ham and eggs arrived and they had to busy themselves buttering bread, pouring tea and, to her surprise, enjoying the food. Ada had been right on one count: Fran was hungry.

At last she was able to speak, but it was not to give the lengthy explanation of her case that she had intended. Instead, she simply said, 'Thank you, Ada. You are a good friend. But you did not see the look on Gowan's face when I last saw him. He can't understand my parents' attitudes. And you didn't hear my mother's words when I told her about him.'

Ada shook her head dismissively. 'I am here for you, my dearest friend, but you must talk to them.'

'Will you come with me to see my mother?'

Ada paused and considered the proposition. She looked grave as she said, 'No, Fran. This is something you should have already done and something you should do alone. Think of your parents. They would not like to know that an outsider knew about the baby before they did. And are you sure of your priorities? It is the child's father who you should approach first! '

It was Fran's turn to consider her response. 'No,' she decided. 'I'll tell my mother first. Please, Ada, you must realise that I've gone against her advice and ignored her opinion. I owe it to her to be honest. And, dear friend, please understand that I'm not sure of Gowan's intentions. He despises my heritage, and I think I was flattered by his attention. I lacked the sense to see beyond an infatuation. I must see my mother first.'

In Whitby, Sarah had been planning. She wanted to impress her other daughters that Fran's liaison with Gowan Pickering was a serious cause for concern. She also wanted to convert Rose from a disinterested bystander to an ally, and Lily into an active participant in the battle.

She had seen the sniggers when Fran had been with them at

Christmas, but her girls had to know that this was no laughing matter. She needed a strategy. She had asked the family for their ideas, and the view seemed to be that Fran should be encouraged to spend Easter with them, but too much pressure would force a rift that would be difficult to heal.

'Surely this is nothing but a silly interlude,' Lily suggested. 'She can't have been walking out with Mr Pickering for long.'

'You're right,' Hannah had agreed. 'We'll try to nip this whole affair in the bud.'

Sarah had composed a letter saying how much they looked forward to seeing Fran at Easter. When a note had arrived from Fran to say she would catch the train on Thursday morning, they looked forward with relative confidence to the Easter weekend; hopefully it would be the end of a difficult episode.

Fran divulged nothing when she first arrived. The talk was of Lily's success with her pupils, and John's in his new venture making colourful waistcoats for wealthy clients. Fran knew she would need to wait for an appropriate moment to speak to her mother.

On Good Friday morning, she joined her family at the morning service, but she found it difficult to maintain an air of normality. Brunswick Street Methodist Church towered high above the road that gave it its name, and its intricate but solid stone architecture suggested to the worshipper a permanence that was comforting.

The organ played quietly as they took their seats, and all eyes focused on the minister. The figure of Christ on the cross, portrayed in a fine oil painting, reminded the onlooker of His suffering. As Fran took her place by Lily's side, she felt the hardness of the wooden pew, the chill in the air. As she prayed, she raised her bowed head to gaze at the scene of sadness that the painting depicted. Christ's body lay limp, cold and bloodied, His lovely head with its gentle curls desecrated by the crown of thorns.

Her eyes roamed to the altar, stripped bare and with the candles unlit. All was sadness. Only a vase of lilies relieved the scene, but even their magnificence only served to impress the onlooker of the loneliness of death, for they represented the tears of Christ who had died for humankind's sins.

In sombre mood, the congregation sang 'The Old Rugged Cross' and 'Rock of Ages, Cleft for Me'. The minister preached a sermon urging his flock to remember the sacrifice and death of Christ and retelling the story of Calvary, the sadness of Jesus being mocked by the crowds and Peter's denial of Him.

Fran shivered as she heard Christ's words 'It is finished' and 'It is done' as the Gospel according to John was read, and she listened more intently than she ever had to Christ's cries from the cross, 'Father forgive them for they know not what they do.' She barely dared look in the preacher's direction as he took 'sin' as his theme and urged his flock to forgive sinners but to refrain from being such themselves.

Even the words of the Lord's Prayer took on a new and personal meaning as she joined the congregation when they recited the words 'Forgive us our trespasses' and 'Lead us not into temptation'. She used the moment of silent prayer to offer her own supplication to Christ and fervently prayed that she might find a solution to her plight, that God might one day forgive her and that she would never again stray from the path of righteousness.

The service ended with the lighter tones of 'There is a Green Hill Far Away' and she joined her family as they left to return to Flowergate.

The service impressed yet further on her mind the depth of her misery. Far from offering comfort to her, the sinner, Fran was left with an intense disgust at her own condition and lack of self-worth.

To Sarah, the occasion was a relief in a strange way. Her wayward daughter had returned; she could look forward to a simple meal appropriate to the day, share this annual period of reflection, and look forward to the happier service of Easter Day. 'Perhaps,' she considered, 'I was too hasty with Fran. She's had time to reflect on her position and surely she's changed her mind.'

They ate when they returned from church and ensured the welfare of the lodgers. At the end of a day that had been more relaxed than a usual Friday, Lily sat at the piano, Hannah and Mary read, John snoozed in his favourite chair and Rose made valiant attempts to work on a tapestry she had designed.

Sarah busied herself in the kitchen preparing supper for the lodgers and Fran took the opportunity to offer to help. 'Oh, Fran! It's been so lovely to have you join us for Easter,' her mother said.

Fran looked unsure of herself.

'Here, make yourself useful, dear.' Sarah gave her daughter a welcoming smile. 'Uncle William's a lovely lodger, but he's taken to his bed. Would you butter some bread and set a tray for him?'

Fran silently did as she was asked. She did not respond to her mother's chatter about the difficulties of ensuring the welfare of ageing lodgers or the delights of seeing a family share their holiday time together. Instead, with shaking hands, she avoided eye contact and at last murmured, 'Mother, I have something I must talk to you about.'

'How lovely!' was Sarah's response.

'I doubt it,' from Fran. 'You won't like what I have to say, Mother.'

'Nonsense!' came the immediate reply. 'It is lovely that you have joined us for this Eastertime. You know we've seen too little of you of late and I think you must be glad of a break from the difficulties of dealing with inclement weather and the challenging conditions at your school. Surely you must miss the pleasures of home life and the company of your family? I'm sorry if I was too outspoken when last we met, but my sentiments were genuine and my concern for your welfare very real.'

Sarah was taken aback at her daughter's reaction. Tears flowed down Fran's cheeks, sobs racked her shoulders and she stopped trying to set Uncle William's tray. She leaned against the edge of the sink, clutched at a tea-towel to mop her face that was now contorted with grief, and looked as if she was about to faint.

Sarah reached forward to support her daughter's shaking body. Horrified, she exclaimed, 'What on earth are you saying, Fran? What could possibly be the cause of this dreadful outburst? Explain yourself.'

In muted tones, scarcely able to raise her eyes and yet relieved that at last she could share her terrible secret, Fran revealed the cause of her distress. The result was cataclysmic.

Sarah received the news in stunned silence. Suddenly, the reason for her daughter's tired features, withdrawn demeanour and reticence about her recent life on the moors became clear. For once, she was speechless and out of her depth. She gazed at her daughter's fragile body as she grappled with her own reaction to the news – horror, anger, fear, shock. But she did nothing and said nothing.

Rose broke the silence. Lent was not part of the Christian calendar that she enjoyed. The meagre rations might be an appropriate precursor to the enjoyment of the more exciting Easter Day feast, but they always left her with a feeling of dissatisfaction. She wondered if her mother's larder might include a slice of cheese, a hot-cross bun or a piece of ham. In search of such a treat, she barged into the kitchen and was greeted by a scene which, she later maintained, never left her memory. Her first reaction was simply to exclaim, 'What on earth's going on here?'

Sarah looked at Fran and said in cold, unfeeling tones, 'Do you want to explain yourself to your sister?'

Fran felt she had little choice and told Rose her secret. This time, she received a very different reaction. 'You stupid girl! You

96

idiot! What possessed you? What are you going to do? Mother, what can we do? Who is the father? Or don't we need to ask? I'll tell the others.'

Rose left. Within seconds, the family was appraised of the situation and the quiet stillness of Good Friday was destroyed as voices were raised and lowered. Each family member offered their opinion on the best way to deal with a crisis that none had expected or previously experienced. Fran felt her downfall was complete.

Rose was the most vociferous. She had a more detailed knowledge of the inmates of the workhouse than the rest of the family, and declared that without a husband and means of support, this was likely to be her sister's destination.

Hannah promptly interjected with a horrified 'No!', and wondered if there were any members of their extended family who could take Fran in. She looked at her father, whose links to his place of birth were tenuous but a possibility.

Mary suggested the baby should be their first consideration, and that there were childless married women who sometimes adopted infants if they could be convinced that the parents were good, practising Christians.

Lily initially took no part in the conversation but, with her connections to the Mission to Seamen, offered the thought that she had heard of women who had met a similar fate to Fran's being sent to the colonies.

Sarah could not be dragged out of her stunned silence, and John waited until his womenfolk had said their piece before he simply said, 'That scoundrel Gowan will have to marry her,' whereupon Sarah took a deep sigh, looked at her ill-fated daughter and resignedly nodded her head in agreement.

TEN

THE DATE OF Easter 1908 had been promising as it fell in the latter half of April when hopes had been high that there would be a warm spring to herald the end of the winter gloom. But intermittent falls of snow caused problems and for once the townsfolk and country people were in agreement; expectations had been disappointed, plans had been thwarted and winter was far from over. However, none of them were prepared for the freak weather conditions that showed their full force immediately after Easter Day and reached their dreadful climax on St George's Day.

Blizzards raged, temperatures plummeted and tales of disaster abounded. Communication ceased as railways stopped running and roads were blocked. Buildings were damaged and livelihoods put at risk as fishing boats, stocks of goods and livestock were destroyed. Individuals faced ruin. Temperatures climbed by the end of the week but torrential rain added further damage to a fragile infrastructure, and talk was of little other than the weather and its mighty power.

On the moors the weather meant a fight for survival, where some would overcome its terrible impact and others would be overwhelmed by its murderous power. Travel between farms and cottages became impossible during the blizzards, and banks of snow up to fifteen feet high were reported across Browside and towards the Flask Inn. Becks stopped flowing as they were caught in the icy grip, and frantic efforts were made to save treasured possessions, keep birds and animals alive, eke out perishable foodstuffs and care for the most vulnerable.

When the torrential downpours combined with melting snow, water found resting places in outhouses, barns and houses. Roofs gave way and hard-won efforts to store vital supplies often came to nothing when destruction followed in the path of nature's wildest and most angry mood.

Gowan Pickering was quick to react to the crisis. The family had missed the Easter Day service at St Stephen's Church for the first time in living memory. As they attempted normality by gathering at Thorney Brow for their annual Easter dinner, he announced that he and Reginald would leave Browside Cottage, move in with the rest of the family and take charge of the emergency.

Jane was delighted. Her youngest son, her pride and joy, would ensure their safety. Henry Newton was equally pleased. Unable to travel to Robin Hood's Bay and his butcher's shop, he felt inadequate to deal with the problems at Thorney Brow. Strong arms, healthy muscles and experienced hands were needed, and Gowan had them all.

That night, the elements threw their worst at Fylingdales. Always prepared to battle to preserve his beloved country, land and family, Gowan worked in a way that others marvelled at. When the blizzards had done their worst, he single-handedly shovelled tons of snow. He carted fodder from the outbuildings to feed sheep that were barely surviving on a rough patch of icy pasture, and spent the evening hours in the stable with his horses, rubbing them down and protecting them with sacking.

He rose early to scarify iron-hard earth to prevent the cattle from slipping and falling, and he manhandled pigs away from crushing each other when their living quarters were reduced in size to allow for extra storage space. When melting snow and driving rain damaged roofing he repaired it, and when drains were blocked with deep, slippery mud he cleared them. None could match the energy and drive that he put into his work.

Reginald and Ernest Harry watched their father in awe; they tried to help as best they could but knew they could not compete. The girls, Elizabeth Estill and Ethel Jane, whispered secretly that they thought their father was the strongest man on earth, and Margaret loved her brother for his mighty support.

At night he ate whatever the womenfolk put on the table for him, warmed his chilled, aching muscles in front of the fire and prepared to work again the next day. Jane worried that he would collapse with fatigue. As the worst of the terrible days ended, she sat in her kitchen one evening and gazed at the face of her son as he slept in his chair. He had outperformed her wildest expectations; he was a man who never accepted defeat, with a fearsome determination that either excited or daunted the onlooker.

'T' lad canna' go on like this,' she murmured. 'He's a fine figure of a man, but he'll age like the rest on us and all this work'll do him no good. He's like a man possessed. He's too much drive, and he's tekkin' out on t' farm whatever angers him. I'll not be there for him forever. T' man needs to take stock of his life. He needs a good woman, a regular home and a steadying influence.'

Lines had appeared on his already rugged features; his gnarled hands, roughened by recent exertion, lay across his wide, muscular chest that only seemed to accentuate his thin, sinuous legs and arms. His hair was showing signs of grey.

'Why should a younger son be the one to cause me restless nights? William and Mary at Low Flask Farm cause me little concern. Poor John's ailing wife is a fearsome problem, but they seem to manage well enough at Hoggarth Hill. And the one that looks the strongest, the one that casts the longest shadow, is the one I grieve for.'

For once, Jane's assessment of her sons' differing situations was ill-judged. As soon as the weather allowed for a semblance of normality, news arrived of John's wife's illness. Already frail, she had found the events of the preceding weeks too great a burden. With only the support of his sickly fourteen-year-old daughter, Rebecca, his son, John William, aged twelve, and the farm servant, George, John Pickering had suffered more than any of the rest of the family.

As soon as it was possible to reach Hoggarth Hill where John and Rebecca farmed, provisions were supplied from Thorney Brow and by William and Mary from Low Flask Farm, but Rebecca did not rally and her condition worsened. At Thorney Brow and Low Flask, voices were muted, eyes downcast, nerves on edge. There was no sign of celebration that the worst of the weather was over.

As the first buds appeared in the hedgerows and the first blades of new grass pushed through the sodden earth, Jane's fears about Gowan's disposition were overshadowed by a greater tragedy on the 16th of May when Rebecca died.

Her funeral was a grim reminder of the service that had commemorated the life of Tamar, which had also left in its wake a widowed man and motherless children. Jane Pickering sat at the front of the church, her head and face veiled in black, her body erect and rigid, her daughter by her side. Gowan and William took up positions on either side of their brother, their families crowding the pews behind them.

The Reverend Chapman received the body and intoned the words, 'We receive the body of our sister, Rebecca, with confidence in God, the giver of life, who raised the Lord Jesus from the dead.'

Little Walter fidgeted and pulled at his black armband, and his older brother, Thomas, quietened him with a meaningful glance. As the service progressed, muffled sobs from John and Rebecca's daughter intermingled with the words, 'I am the resurrection and the life, says the Lord. Those who believe in me, even though they die, will live.'

At the back of the church, neighbours, business associates, servants and farm workers paid their respects. The Donkins from Robin Hood's Bay sat together in a gesture of solidarity; the Noble family joined their son, George, who had married one of John Pickering's daughters, and the Harlands brought little Alice, Rebecca's niece. George Carter and his family had travelled from Carlin How, where Pickerings, Harlands and Carters had gone to work at the blast furnaces. Fylingdales was saying farewell to one of its own.

Rebecca's wake was held at Thorney Brow. As Jane took up her position as family matriarch, the family gradually settled. The youngsters remained in the kitchen, their parents and older siblings in the parlour. The tension of the day began to recede; for the first time since the onset of the dreadful days of snow, the horrors of the deluge and the sadness of Rebecca's illness, conversation was no longer restrained and voices no longer muted. The funeral had served its purpose and provided a fitting conclusion to a life. Now those left behind were allowed to plan for the future.

'Tha'll not be able to manage Hoggarth Hill now,' said Gowan to his grieving brother. 'Yon child of yours is like her mother and needs a care that you'll not be able to give. What plans have you made?'

John faced the inevitable. 'She'll be off to Carlin How to live wi' her sister.' He looked drawn and tired, his skin grey. The previous weeks of turmoil had taken their toll on his health.

Unsurprised, Gowan greeted the news with resignation. His son, John Clark interjected. 'Me and me cousin allus' shared a fancy to move away from t' land. We both live at Carlin now and like it well enough. The ironworks there pay us, and we're not far from where Rebecca will stay. We'll keep an eye on her. But what about you and young John William, Uncle?'

'I've put me life into Hoggarth Hill, lad. But it's not to be. I'll work the land, but not the same land and not so hard, I think,' replied John. 'I'll tek a cottage at Normanby for t' lad and me. I've already agreed it wi' t' owner. 'Tis the only way.' He put his head in his hands and the conversation ended.

William and Gowan looked at each other and then at their brother, and an unspoken message spread across the room. There was now an understanding that the Pickerings no longer farmed land as far as the eye could see, and the mourning was not only for the loss of Rebecca but also for the loss of a way of life.

John turned to his brother. 'Are ye back at Browside, Gowan?' he enquired.

'Ay. I did what was needed here for the crisis, but it'll be a while before the wreckage from the storms is properly dealt with. Browside took a beating. 'Tis barely fit to live in, but there's only Reginald and me there now so we manage well enough. It could be worse. T' breeding stock for t' pigs and sheep are safe and t' horses lived, thank God. For now, we'll finish t' repairs and rebuild when we can.'

'Tha'll tek a break before that, lad!' interrupted Jane. Turning to William, she tried to recruit him as an ally. 'Tha' brother's exhausted, William. Knock some sense into him. Tell him to stop killing himself. T' land's not going anywhere. It'll still be here to tend long after we've all gone.'

William laughed. 'Since when did Gowan tek any heed of my advice?' But he turned to his brother and his face was serious when he remarked, 'Be honest, brother. Tha' looks exhausted and I reckon tha's lost weight. For once, tek a bit of advice and try to relax.'

'There!' Jane smiled at William. 'Even tha' brother thinks like me for once. Tek' heed, Gowan.'

Margaret interjected. 'We all care for thee, Gowan. We all

want to see you fit and tha' should be honest; tha's overdone it of late.'

Gowan glared at them all. The preceding weeks had taken their toll, and he knew it, but he believed the answer to his fatigue lay in the land. He hated the overheated, overcrowded parlour, the chatter, the need to feed extra mouths in the kitchen. He loathed the need to be welcoming and polite to guests – he detested the thought that his brother's loss of Hoggarth Hill meant the Pickerings were no longer master of all they surveyed. He longed to escape from the rituals of mourning, to leave gossip to the womenfolk, leave the overfull farmhouse and escape from the constant sadness of the day and the dreary business of catering for the bereaved.

He rose to his feet, mockingly proffered his glass of gin in silent cheer, and then raised his resonant voice above the general hubbub. 'I'll be master of my own destiny and I'll thank you all for minding thy own business. When I want thy advice, I'll ask for it, and when tha' all live perfect lives, I'll listen to thee. And now, I'll wish thee all good-day for I've had enough o' mournin', if it means a constant criticism.'

The room fell silent. William and Mary's sons, Gowan, William, Christopher and Jack stood like statues. Reginald and Ernest Harry looked embarrassed. Henry Newton sidled over to Margaret in a gesture of support. Jane remained her usual immutable self but tensed at the prospect of family disharmony.

Gowan left the assembled company and stormed out into the bright spring air. He breathed deeply and savoured the smell of the moors. He strode to the field next to the house and Kitty walked to greet him straight away. He stroked her fine coat and ran his fingers across the soft, downy hair around her ears. She nuzzled his hand, and her warmth invited him to join her. Bareback, he walked her round the field and, as he did so, the stress of the day began to leave him.

He decided to leave the wake, leave the problems of land, children, work and the impossible questions about the future. His salvation was not amongst the grieving or amongst the rituals of death; it lay across the moors. He saddled Kitty, collected his crop from an outhouse and rode out from Thorney Brow.

The sun was setting and birds were starting their late-afternoon symphony as Gowan rode across his beloved earth. The absence of human companionship, the solitude of open spaces and the undisciplined juxtaposition of heather, moss and lichen revived his aching limbs and soothed his melancholy. His figure became more erect, and a vibrancy that had been lacking as energy had been sapped by the preceding weeks returned. Here was life in the midst of death, nature at her most glorious. Here, there was no mourning but the joy of new life.

He skirted Howdale Farm and climbed the incline of Brow Moor. He walked Kitty past rough-hewn stone gouged from the earth by quarrymen and on to Stoupe Brow, where the taste of salt in the air and the sound of the gentle swell of the sea tempted him to higher ground. At the sight of the ocean and its endless vista, he stopped and breathed deeply.

He set Kitty to a trot and then to a canter as the ground levelled off near the edge of the cliffs. The wind caught his hair and his jacket billowed out behind him. He kicked his heels into the horse's flesh and she responded with a joyous bound. As they galloped across the land, man and horse as one, both released from the imprisonment of catastrophe, he let out a loud 'Hulloo'. And when their flight was over, he slowed his mount, returned her to a gentle trot and whispered in her ear, ''Tis time I saw t' little schoolma'am.'

Gowan released his horse on the coarse, moss-riven grass outside the schoolhouse. Inside, Fran was preparing to leave. As she buttoned up her coat, cast a glance at the ashes in the stove to check they were safe and turned towards the door, it was flung open. She jumped and let out a sharp cry.

'I caught thee unawares, little schoolma'am!' chuckled Gowan. 'I've neglected thee of late and am come to make amends. Tell me you can spare some of your time to humour me, for I'm in need of comfort after these terrible days.'

Fran recovered quickly from her shock but, to Gowan's chagrin, was far from welcoming in her greeting. 'What possesses you to seek me out on this of all days? Why are you not with your family? I've wanted to speak to you, but wouldn't dream of intruding on a family so bereft. Surely they have greater need of you than you have of me!'

Gowan looked annoyed. Impatiently, he struck the side of one of the little schoolroom chairs with his riding crop. 'Am I to go away? Are you rejecting my offer of a renewed friendship between us? If that's the case, I'll leave. It'll be your choice.'

Fran's response was less than clear as she fumbled for words in her confusion. 'No,' she said, 'I don't want you to go away. I want you to stay because I've an urgent reason to talk to you and I've wanted to do so for some time. I don't want you to leave, but I didn't expect you. You can't have recovered from the winter yet, and you've barely laid poor Rebecca to rest. I'm unsure of myself, lost for words. I want you to listen and I want you to brace yourself for information you might not welcome. Don't go. I must explain myself.'

Gowan looked puzzled. 'Tha' looks very serious, lass. Is it bad news concerning your family? Are your parents or sisters sick, or is it that the snow and then the rain have left disaster in their wake? Tell me. My family has suffered enough, but the people of Whitby have suffered too. Have your family been amongst the casualties?'

Fran fell silent, her face a mixture of agitation and quivering uncertainty. As if to dispel the tension that now pervaded the air, Gowan sat on one of the school desks, his long legs sprawled in front of him. He demanded, 'Speak up, lass. Tha' knows my quarrel has not been so much wi' thee as wi' thy parents. They are the ones who vex me. And tha's right defending them, even if tha' doesn't agree with everything they say. I shouldn't ha' been so hard on thee when we had our quarrel. But if tha' has sommat to say, speak up! I hope I can still be tha' friend, and friends should be there to help each other.'

Fran took a deep breath. She had prepared her speech many times, rehearsed this moment in her mind, but now she felt inadequate to the task. She hesitated, but at last she spoke in a quiet voice. In what she hoped was a dignified tone, she said the words she had waited to say: 'I am pregnant.'

Gowan made no response. He drew up his legs and sat upright, but his shoulders stooped, his earlier joviality disappeared and a weariness seemed to overwhelm him. His face turned ashen and his hands lay limp across his lap.

Fran studied his face; he was a shadow of the man she once knew. She saw the lines and furrows of distress, the posture of defeat. In the silence, she dare not question his intent or press her cause; instead, she prayed he might somehow summon the strength to help her.

She could no longer feel the vibrancy of his character or the power of his presence. Even her parents had agreed that the Pickerings had suffered more than most in recent times and that an approach to Gowan had to be delayed until the healing power of time had run its course. Here in front of her was evidence that time had not run its course; she knew that her news had presented a challenge that appeared to be Gowan's final undoing. She wanted to soothe him, banish his weariness, but she suffered the miasma of a room where the outside world seemed no longer to exist and felt only her own impotence.

At last Gowan raised himself from his torpor. 'Well, there's a pretty fix!' he said. 'I had not prepared for this.' He rose and looked through the window past Kitty, grazing contentedly, and across the rough acres.

His old self revived momentarily as, with a guffaw, he remarked, 'And what do thy parents think to a blackguard like me fathering their grandchild? I doubt they're best pleased!' Then he suggested they leave the schoolroom and walk across the land.

She agreed. She closed the door behind her and he led the way in silence along the path that led towards Browside Cottage. Open ground gave occasional glimpses of the now-quiet sea. Green shoots were breaking through the dark earth as nature gradually worked its magic.

Gowan lost some of his pallor and walked erect and with purpose. He told Fran that he wanted her to see his home but that she must be prepared for a shock. She was puzzled. He had looked traumatised when she told him of her pregnancy and had implied no willingness to acknowledge the baby publicly as his. The long wait to confront him had ended without a conclusion and her fears for the future were no less now than they had been, no nearer an acceptable resolution. She decided not to question him and waited.

When they arrived, the sight was sufficient explanation for Gowan's warning. Fran gasped at what she saw. The roof was damaged to such an extent that it barely covered the building, and the chimney hung precariously above stone supports that were once the internal stack but were now exposed to the elements. Windows were broken. Although the door was intact, it was of questionable value without a fully formed building to protect; it offered neither security nor shelter. All around was debris from the wild ravages of the winter storms.

Her voice quivered as she blurted out, 'I can't believe that you and Reginald live here! How do you manage? Where do you sleep? Where do you eat? Surely this can never be put right! Oh,

I am so sorry. I knew you'd suffered, but I hadn't realised how much.'

Gowan reached out and put a comforting arm around her shoulders. 'Now, little schoolma'am, I think you understand a little better t' reasons for my depression. And perhaps you will better understand my reticence when tha' gave me tha' news. I'm a man of honour and I'll marry thee, Fran. You'll understand that I had a mind to anyway. But tha'll also understand I've no home to offer you.

'One day, this cottage'll be repaired. I'll do it me'sen, but this is not a job that'll be done in a hurry. I made sure my family was cared for when t' weather chose to inflict its worst on us, and I make no apologies for my decision to put their welfare above all else. But during my absence from this place, no human hand was here to check nature's wildest moods. Now, I must deal wi' t' consequences.

'Look at me, Fran and be honest. Are you not looking at a changed man? I never felt inadequate before and was always in control of my destiny. Now, the prospect of another family to care for, more mouths to feed, new responsibilities, daunts me. Yes, I was shocked when tha' spoke to me, and no, I had not expected what tha' told me and my mind was not at its most receptive. But now I think we'll have to deal wi' t' predicament as best we can. If I am to be a father again, there'll have to be some decisions made. And, if I'm honest, I canna' see an easy way to make 'em.'

They did not stay long at Browside Cottage. The evening air was chilly, and Gowan needed to take Kitty back to her stable at Thorney Brow and face the repercussions from his mother following his untimely departure earlier in the day. For the moment, there was little more to say, and they parted with an agreement that they would speak again the following week.

On her return to the Pettys' cottage, Fran packed a bag ready for the weekend and prepared herself for a difficult interview with her family.

The Booths were anxiously awaiting news from the moors. There had been some disagreement about the need to shelter the Pickerings from knowledge of Fran's pregnancy but it had been accepted that, whilst the initial intention to approach Gowan had been thwarted by the weather, common decency dictated that no approach be made to him until after Rebecca's funeral. Now the funeral had taken place and Fran could approach him with impunity. Her future could be decided.

When she arrived at 50 Flowergate, Lily was at a rehearsal of the Whitby Choral Society, Hannah was nursing Mary who was unwell after catching a chill during the winter rains, and John was clearing unwanted scraps of fabric and thread from the basement ready for the rag-and-bone man to collect. Fran was relieved. Her mother was alone in the kitchen and they could talk without interruption.

Sarah greeted her daughter with her usual offer of a cup of tea. Her mouth smiled, but her eyes were full of uncertainty and apprehension. Barely had they sat down at the kitchen table than she asked, 'Have you spoken to Mr Pickering?'

'Yes.'

'And what was the outcome? Will he behave honourably? Will he marry you?'

'Yes.'

'Oh, Fran.' Sarah sighed. 'I didn't ask for a man like him to take you from us, but at least I can thank God that you are to be provided for and your baby will have a name. When will you marry? I assume some attention must be paid to the period of mourning. When do you think will be appropriate?' She did not look pleased, but she looked relieved.

She put her arm on her daughter's shoulder. With a reassuring hug, she said, 'We will still be here for you, you know. And I think this is the best outcome we can expect.'

Fran hesitated, unsure of her response. How could she explain to her mother that the Pickerings' problems were far greater than a sad death in the family?

'I can't answer your question, Mother. Gowan has said we will marry, but the winter has wrought havoc on him and his family and he's living in a place that can barely be described as a home. It lacks the basic necessities, the roof has caved in, the structure of the building has lost its integrity, and he faces months of hard effort to repair it. At the moment, there is nowhere for us to live. Poor Gowan and Reginald live in a way that almost defies my ability to describe it. It's all so sad.'

'Well, that's it! I knew the people of the moors lived like animals, and now the very man who every God-fearing person would agree should marry you has proved me right! He and his son do live like animals. Fran, this situation gets worse.' Sarah looked distraught. 'What are we to do? You can't possibly live like that, especially in your condition. And how would you care for a baby?' She slammed the kettle on the stove. 'Oh, how I wish you'd never met that dreadful man.'

Fran rose to Gowan's defence. 'Mother! How could you be so cruel? Gowan did not ask for this terrible situation. The fact that he was caring for his family took him away from his own and Reginald's needs. You should respect a man who gives so much, asks so little and suffers for his efforts.'

'Respect?' interjected Sarah. 'I think your opinion is biased, my girl. I'll never respect a man who subjects his eldest son to the ignominy of living in unacceptable discomfort and who offers marriage but, in the same breath, makes sure he cannot fulfil the requirements of the married state. He is no more than a charlatan.'

Fran's face flushed. Her whole being quivered, and she was about to give a feisty reply when Hannah joined them. She started to explain that Mary was breathing more comfortably, but stopped in her tracks. 'What is happening?' she asked.

Sarah slammed her hand down on the table. 'Well, Fran, you can tell your sister! Let her hear Mr Pickering's attempts to avoid his responsibilities. Convince her your life will be improved by marrying a man who lives in a barn.'

'Tell her yourself!' Fran turned her face away from her mother. 'Whatever I say means nothing.'

Hannah, uncomfortable and fearful, asked, 'What's happening? Tell me. Has Gowan refused you?'

'No.' Fran was quick to correct her. 'It's Mother who refuses to understand Gowan's predicament. Her mind's so set against him that no words of mine will mollify her. He will marry me, but his home was destroyed by the winter's onslaught and we have nowhere to live.'

Hannah was about to respond when Lily arrived. The beauty of Handel's work always lifted her spirits. She had been rehearsing what to her was the greatest of his works, Messiah, and in particular 'I Know That My Redeemer Liveth'. To her, the gentle but powerful words, the glorious harmony, the sweet message of redemption were all the rationale for music.

The contrast was stark as she entered the kitchen of 50 Flowergate, yet the music still rang in her ears. The sight of the one sister with whom she had always shared her passions, the one with whom she had the greatest empathy, sitting with a look of utter hopelessness on her face, stirred her into action. She ignored the strained atmosphere and the looks of anger and tension. She reached out to Fran, put her arms around her sister and said, 'I know it's not long since you returned to the moors, but I have so missed you, Fran. I need to know that you are well. Tell me your news.'

Lily's gesture broke the deadlock. Sarah adopted a posture of defeat; Hannah reached for the kettle; Fran quietly, and without rancour, explained her predicament again. This time, a more reasoned discussion could take place.

'It's not the fact that Mr Pickering and his son are living the way they do, it is because winter on the moors is so destructive,' said Hannah. 'I dread the thought of Fran leaving us for a life so terrifying. And with a baby! What if there is another dreadful winter next year? What if Mr Pickering repairs his cottage, but the roof falls in with her underneath it?'

'You know that is most unlikely. And anyway, it can't be repaired so quickly that it would be ready for a new family,' insisted Fran.

'What about his existing family? Are they without a roof over their heads?' queried Hannah.

'No, that is why his own home is so neglected. They are safe. Thorney Brow is housing and supporting them all, thanks to Gowan's efforts.'

'Thanks to Gowan, indeed!' an affronted Sarah chipped in. 'Since when did anyone thank a good-for-nothing, self-opinionated, egocentric moors man for allowing his house to be destroyed and for forcing his son to live in worse conditions than his horse?'

Sarah's outburst forced Lily to speak more decisively. 'She can't go! She must stay here. She must marry Gowan to secure her baby's future, but she can't live with its father, at least for now. Would you condemn your daughter to such a fate? Would you force her out of her home knowing she had nowhere to go?'

Turning to Fran, she shrugged her shoulders. 'I don't think you are in a position to choose, Fran. You must accept hospitality wherever it is offered and, in my opinion, it should be here.'

Fran had no answers, no suggestions to make. She, Hannah and Lily all looked at their mother, but none could decide what she was thinking.

At last, Sarah said, 'There's many a family taken in their

kinsfolk. I know of babies and children reared by grandparents, aunts and cousins, but usually it's the result of death or ill-health. Mr Pickering is very much alive and well. Are we to care for a daughter and a new baby simply because he wants to shirk his responsibilities? Where would Fran and her baby sleep? How could I carry on my lodging house with fewer rooms to spare? Are we to support Mr Pickering's offspring, with all the problems that would bring, while he lives his life unencumbered? Lily, your kindly attitude to your sister is laudable but I don't think you've thought through the implications of your suggestion.'

'I think you should talk to Father,' said Hannah.

That night Fran lay in the bed she shared with Lily and wished that sleep would come. The lamplighter had done his work and snuffed out the street lights. No shadows played on the curtains, no moon illuminated the dark recesses of the room, and the horsehair mattress suddenly seemed hard and uncomfortable.

Lily had feigned exhaustion when they went to bed and refused to talk. Now, she was sleeping and the soft, regular sound of her breathing gave comfort in the cold chill of the room, but her presence also reminded Fran that even her closest ally was no supporter of Gowan.

Fran was tired, but the sounds of laughter and the muffled conversations of late-night revellers leaving the nearby public house disturbed the quiet of the outside world, and inside the house she could hear the muted tones of her parents' voices. Tomorrow, she would learn of their decision.

ELEVEN

IN JULY 1908, there was to be a wedding at Brunswick Road Methodist Church, Whitby. Fran's parents had agreed to her marriage and Fannie Elizabeth Booth was to become Mrs Gowan Hodgson Pickering.

On the appointed day, Gowan and William sat together waiting for the bride's arrival. Both wished they were back on the moors, squirming with discomfort in suits that were reserved for weddings, funerals and baptisms. Both abhorred the Nonconformist lack of ornamentation, the interminable sermons and what they viewed as the smug self-righteousness of the tradesmen, industrialists and artisans who frequented this church but they felt wouldn't last five minutes on the moors.

Behind them were Jane, Margaret with her husband Henry, and Reginald. Reginald and Henry gave no indication of their thoughts, but Jane and Margaret were deep in hushed conversation and both looked delighted at the prospect of the forthcoming marriage.

'There's me looking for a wife for Gowan amongst us farming folk!' Jane said. 'I canna' say I'd ha' thought of a little schoolma'am as a suitable wife, but that young Miss Booth'll mek a fine mother to Gowan's children. She'll learn t' ways of t' farm, for she's not lacking understanding. 'Tis a weight off my mind to see Gowan settled again.'

Margaret smiled. 'T' lass'll need some support, I think! I've not properly met them yet, but I'm told her mother and sisters are against the match and only accepted it because of the baby.

We'll look at their faces and see if they're likely to cause trouble. T' last thing newlyweds need is friction in their families, and t' last thing Gowan needs is criticism after all he's gone through. Not that he'll tek it off the likes of them!'

Their conversation was cut short by the arrival of the Booth family and the loud and glorious sound of the organ as it suddenly burst forth with Wagner's *Lohengrin*. A radiant Fran had arrived, accompanied by her father.

The vicar performed his duties, vows were exchanged, a simple gold wedding ring was placed on Fran's finger and prayers were said. After what Reginald considered was a completely unnecessary monologue from the vicar on the sanctity of marriage, the couple were pronounced man and wife.

The wedding party left the church and retired to 50 Flowergate for a simple wedding breakfast. Sherry, tiny sandwiches, and the traditional wedding cake were offered, and John made a hesitant but genuine toast to the bride and groom. In a gruff but resounding voice, Gowan thanked his new parents-in-law for their hospitality and gave his bride words of praise. Lily played the piano, Sarah, Hannah and Mary made tea. Rose embarked on a conversation about Henry Campbell-Bannerman resigning the premiership in favour of Herbert Asquith, leaving Jane baffled as to why she was so concerned with politics.

Fran and Gowan barely spoke other than in whispers. Only when Gowan leaned over and said, 'Tha's a pretty spectacle and no mistake,' did Fran confirm to herself that this was the man she wanted. This was her dream. Her baby would be born at 50 Flowergate, but she knew Gowan would prepare a home for them as soon as he could. Her future was secure.

The wedding party broke up in time for the Pickerings to catch a train back to the moors. Gowan left with them, acutely aware of his enforced separation from his new wife. The Booth family had been cordial to him and his family, but he knew he was beholden to them.

He was angry; he saw his beautiful bride and a chance to make a new life for himself and his children, but until he could provide a home, he must suffer the indignity of meeting his wife as a visitor. He would have to accept the dictates of his in-laws and be deprived of the comforts of the married state whilst paying for the privilege. Sarah had made it obvious that Fran's return to Flowergate would cost her dearly in terms of lost income from lodgers. When Gowan felt obliged to offer help, she had accepted without hesitation, remarking that it was the least he could do. He noticed that even on his wedding day, provision had been made for holidaymakers from Leeds, a Mr and Mrs Day, to use the back room of the house because they were paying guests.

'Strangers constantly in the home,' he muttered to himself as he sat in the train carriage. 'No privacy or attempt to prevent nosey, impertinent outsiders from intruding on a day that should be for the family. They do not understand a way of life that puts food on their table and will offer their daughter a fine future – and no liking for the most basic requirements of a decent wedding with all that silly Nonconformist nonsense. And all set in the smoky, filthy air of an overcrowded, poverty-stricken town.'

Jane and Margaret were sitting in the same carriage, and the two women exchanged meaningful looks. They had enough experience of son and brother to know when to keep their counsel. Gowan would not let a situation that obviously grieved him last any longer than he had to. He would work and make Browside Cottage habitable; he would do what he always did and use every fibre of his being to solve his problem.

Although she said nothing, Jane grieved for her son. He was forty-two, past his prime and showing signs of age. He would be tested yet again, and yet again he would rise above adversity, but she wondered how much more he could take.

◆ ◆ ◆

The months that followed were very different for Fran and Gowan. In Whitby, Fran reacquainted herself with old habits. She frequented the markets and was reminded of long-forgotten friends who, like her, had seen changes in their lives. Girls she had played with were now grown women, some with children of their own; boys who had teased her, pulled her hair and rudely displayed themselves in the harbour, where they had swum until the town council had banned swimming naked, were now working men.

Many of the shopkeepers were new to the town, and they offered an exotic mix of languages and products. She familiarised herself with immigrant shopkeepers like the Spiegelhalters, who advertised in the *Whitby Gazette* for 'old gold', and with skilled men who understood electricity and encouraged people to change their gas or oil lighting to electric.

There were ladies who took advantage of women's problems by selling Southalls sanitary towels to the well-off, and chemists who took the place of expensive doctors by diagnosing and treating a wide range of maladies, often with the universal panacea of Beecham's Pills.

She started to fit into Whitby life in a way she had never previously done and she was happy. Her place in society was now decided and her future was secure. Her health was good and her features relaxed; onlookers felt they were in the presence of a woman at peace with the world. As her mother remarked, 'Being pregnant suits you, dear. It's a long time since I've seen you so happy to be with us.'

Gowan was less enamoured of the summer and autumn of 1908. As soon as labour on the land eased, he returned to

Browside Cottage to work on its refurbishment. His home was still a ruin; no matter how many hours he worked, or how much effort he put in, farming took up so much of his time and energy that progress was painfully slow.

Jane hoped that the harvest festival would improve his temper. Under pressure from his family, he dutifully attended St Stephen's and sat with his children as the choir sang 'Fear Not, O Land'. His dead wife's father, Stephen, sang the solo; far from rejoicing at the old man's fine voice and the magnificent display of produce that adorned the church, the event deepened Gowan's depression.

'Onward Christian Soldiers' served to further darken his mood as he weighed the effort he put into his work against the poor outcome. When the service finally ended, he returned to his work at Browside instead of joining his family for the traditional harvest supper.

No-one could change Gowan's mood. Reginald tried to help but, no matter how hard he tried, his work was never good enough for his father. Henry Newton admitted that he was a good butcher but a poor builder. William tried to help his brother but was hard pressed to leave his own family for the agricultural demands were heavy on his time, just as they were on Gowan's.

However, the harvest festival proved a turning point for Gowan in a way that no one had expected.

John Pickering sat quietly at the back of the church. Since the death of his wife, Rebecca, his life had been in turmoil. Left with only his young son, and having given up his farm, he was a lonely figure. He lived with his grief. Seeing Gowan shocked him. His brother's tall, commanding presence had been replaced by a shadow of the man.

John made no move to join the rest of his family after the service, but the next day he went to Browside. Without any instruction from Gowan, he started work on the joists that needed repairing on the upper floor.

Gowan eventually found time to leave the land. He thought he would find his house empty, as he had left it; if anyone was likely to be there to help him, it would be Reginald. He was surprised to see his brother hard at work. 'What inspired this?' he asked gruffly.

'Tha' looks as if tha' could do wi' a bit o' help,' came the reply.

'Tha's not wrong there!'

They said nothing more. Although the two men did not resemble each other in appearance, in many other respects they were alike. Both had the Pickering streak of independence and stubbornness that made them excellent workmen and valuable allies but poor losers. Both viewed work as the solution to life's vicissitudes.

They became a team and started to plan the refurbishment together and, as they shared hard physical labour, they also shared their problems. They recognised that Browside would not be ready for a new family by Christmas, and John was aware of Gowan's frustration that his new life was an unhappy compromise.

John encouraged his brother to visit Fran and to revise his opinion that his time was better spent working on the house. He pointed out that Fran should know the truth about their situation and be told that Browside was far from complete, but she also needed reassurance that Gowan still cared for her.

In turn, Gowan encouraged John to spend time with his son. As he pointed out, the lad had been deprived of a mother and a home; he did not need to be deprived of a father as well. The brothers forged a bond that neither would admit had been needed, but which helped both through dark days of adversity and helped them deal with their problems more effectively.

As November chilled the morning air and winter winds

sprang up, Fran was near her due date. There was a palpable tension in the air in Flowergate. She went into labour in the early hours of Monday, 9th November. John went to the station where the station master agreed to transmit the news to Thorney Brow via his stopping point at Fyling Hall station. Mary was dispatched to break the news to Hannah, who had been helping at the Arundale's public house, and Rose was told to take Lily out; at seventeen, she was too young to be involved.

To Fran, her labour seemed interminable. Pain racked her body, sapped her strength and she felt feverish and light-head as she lay on her bed. The ticking of George, the grandfather clock in the hall, seemed to have no influence on the movement of its hands as time dragged interminably.

As morning turned into afternoon, the tea that her mother made simply induced nausea, but finally she felt she needed to push her baby into the world. Her piercing screams rent the air and John heard the sound from his basement shelter. His hands shook, and he wept.

Finally, the ordeal was over. When Fran felt she could bear no more, her baby was born. Sarah's capable hands deftly caught the tiny body, dealt with the umbilical cord and the afterbirth, and wiped the baby clean. The newborn infant let out a lusty cry.

The effect of the sound of an infant's cry on the family at 50 Flowergate was transformative. When Sarah, hot and exhausted, appeared at the parlour door to announce that mother and a baby boy were well, the tension disappeared.

Gowan arrived as the long day ended. He had ridden to the station, left his horse with the stationmaster and caught the first available train. He entered the house breathlessly and with a worried frown, but received the news that he had another son with obvious pleasure.

In the parlour, the baby's good health was toasted. For the

first time since she had known Gowan, Sarah felt almost at ease. The atmosphere was relaxed, the baby and Fran were well, and the conversation was constructive.

The Booths wanted the child to be called Herbert. In their opinion, the recently appointed Liberal government was inaugurating a new era of care for the most vulnerable in society, and they revered their Prime Minister, Herbert Henry Asquith. Gowan had no objection, for Asquith was a Yorkshireman who firmly rejected female emancipation and was noted for traits that Gowan admired: hard work, tenacity, resilience and independence. For once, Booths and Pickerings were in agreement and set aside their political differences.

Religious differences meant that Gowan insisted the baby should be baptised in the Anglican Church and that was also agreed, but the atmosphere changed when Gowan made his next request. He said he would appreciate it if Sarah could ask the vicar to set a date for Fran's churching.

She was horrified. 'But that's a papist practice!' she retorted. 'I really don't think I could do that, dear.'

'So you'll not give thanks for her safe recovery from childbirth? I think you Nonconformists have lost the meaning of religion!' Gowan replied, obviously annoyed. 'Why, even the lowest labourer on the moors would never fail to offer thanks to God at a time like this. What makes you think you are so special?'

'We don't think of ourselves as special!' It was Sarah's turn to show her irritation. 'But I think we shouldn't be confused with papists and their showy displays of meaningless ritual.' She tried to calm herself. 'Gowan, we do not want to fall out with you, and we will do everything in our power to care for your wife and son, but I think we should draw the line at this. Accept that John and I will have a christening in your church, but please don't ask more of us.'

Gowan was angry. 'You will do everything in your power to care for my wife and son!' he spluttered. 'I should think so. 'Tis your daughter and your grandson we're talking about. As we speak, my mother and sister are caring for my children. That's what families do, woman!'

John had remained silent throughout this exchange, but his expression showed his feelings when Gowan referred to Sarah as 'woman'. 'I'll ask you to show some respect for my wife, sir.' he said.

'I'll respect you both when you start to respect me,' Gowan replied. 'Meanwhile, I'll ask you to fulfil my request, and I'll wish you good-day before I say anything I might regret.'

Gowan slammed his glass down on a small, mahogany side table that rocked unsteadily, collected his coat and left without a backward glance.

Sarah heaved a sigh and turned her tired, drawn features to her husband. 'John, I really don't understand that man. There's no limit to his arrogance, his ignorance, his pomposity. How can a man like that father such a beautiful little baby? What made our daughter want to be with him? What shall we do?'

John remained silent but brooding. As often happened, Sarah answered her own question. 'I think we'll do as the man asks and let him have his church services, but we'll make sure we're very much a part of our grandson's life. He will need our influence to make sure he's not bullied into being a copy of his father.' She hesitated and then added, 'But I think we'll not say too much about this to poor Fran.'

TWELVE

In July 1914 Whitby was thriving. Warm summer sun attracted visitors and boarding houses, hotels, gift shops, pleasure boat operators, cab drivers and hawkers were doing a brisk trade. Bands played on the Promenade, the 'Gay Cadets' performed three times daily on the sands and there were two Battery Parades. Day trippers added to the throng, and the accents acquired in cities and towns accessible by train but unfamiliar to local and often untravelled people gave a cosmopolitan air. The town was at its noisy, lively, colourful best.

In Flowergate, the Booth family felt sheltered from Whitby's most vibrant season. Surrounded by workers and tradesmen, theirs was a place used by the indigenous population rather than visitors and, here, Sarah continued her roles as matriarch and lodging-house keeper, John's tailoring business in the basement thrived; Lily taught music; Hannah continued her dressmaking and Mary, her health always indifferent, helped her mother. Rose had married and lived in Easterby's Yard at the rear of 50 Flowergate and, now, an integral part of the family was Herbert, a lively five year old and John and Sarah's pride and joy.

When, in the autumn of 1909, Gowan had completed the renovation of Browside Cottage, Fran and Herbert moved to their new home and it was here that Kathleen and Annie were born. Fran coped with the day to day running of Browside but found it difficult. Always the optimist, Gowan simply assumed that she would 'soon be back to her old self', but she knew that childbirth had drained her energy. Thus, when Sarah suggested

Herbert be enrolled at Cliff Street School in Whitby and that he should live with the Booth family at Flowergate during term time, Fran was delighted at the idea. Gowan had been less enthusiastic, but agreed on the basis that he would return when Fran's health improved and he was old enough to make his own way to the little Howdale School that had once been his mother's domain.

On the last Sunday of July, the family gathered for their traditional Sunday roast. As Sarah stirred flour into the meat juices in her roasting pan, Rose appeared at the back door. 'Can George and I join you?' She hovered uncertainly.

'What's gone wrong this time?' Sarah's voice had a resigned note.

'Oh, nothing really, Mother, but we haven't got the money for meat this week and, anyway, you know I miss our Sundays together.'

Sarah added cabbage water to the gravy she was making and sighed. 'Have you paid the rent?'

'Yes.'

'Has that husband of yours done any work this week?'

'A little. But it's hard starting your own business – you should know that!'

'You and George have been married nearly four years now, and he started his carpentry business before you married, Rose! How long are you going to keep up this pretence that George can run his own business? And the fact that you are my next-door neighbour does not mean that I have to feed you both.' Sarah slammed the roasting dish onto the draining board and reached for a gravy boat.

As Rose handed it to her with a pleading look, Hannah walked in on the scene and began to set trays that were needed for the lodgers' lunches.

'Easterby's Yard not good enough for you, Rose?'

Rose blushed. 'My house is perfectly adequate, thank you, Hannah, and my husband is doing his best to make it as pleasant as possible. You're only jealous because you haven't got a home of your own.'

Sarah felt herself getting angry. She wanted Sunday to be a day of peace, not a scene of warfare. Her face was stern, and her words ended the discussion. 'You and George will be welcome to join us, Rose dear. Hannah, as soon as you've set those trays, will you please tell Mary to put away the scraps that Herbert and she have been pasting in his scrapbook and make him wash his hands? And will you both then leave me in peace? I have dinner to cook.'

Hannah did as she was asked in silence, Rose left to fetch George, Lily returned from the Mission to Seamen where she had been playing the organ for their morning worship and Mary, helped by an enthusiastic Herbert, replaced the clutter on the dining room table with a cloth, cutlery, serviettes and cruet. The family assembled and John, sitting at the head of the table, thanked the Lord for the food they were about to eat and Sarah thanked Him for a bit of peace.

The rest of the day was uneventful. Lily offered to take Herbert to the promenade where a brass band was playing, but the little boy protested that he wanted to finish his jigsaw and, after lunch, the family sat in the parlour.

John was reading the *Whitby Gazette*. He gave little indication of his feelings, but Sarah had an idea that he rather enjoyed having another man in the house, and she knew George idolised his father-in-law. Thus, when John remarked that the town council was encouraging the populace to kill flies, George was quick to show an interest by, quite unnecessarily, pointing out that flies carried disease. Rose supported her husband by recounting an occasion when she had bought meat from a street hawker whose prices had been tempting but whose meat, she discovered, was full of maggots. Sarah's look of horror was enough to show her dislike of the idea of buying from hawkers, but Rose pointed out that she'd removed the maggots, she and George had eaten the meat and there were some people in Whitby who couldn't even afford that level of luxury.

Hannah looked annoyed. 'And there are some people who simply eat their parents' food when they can't afford their own,' she remarked.

'Please, Hannah, stop being so critical,' rebuked Lily. 'Rose is our sister and we love her. Would you rather she and George starved?'

'I'd rather George did some work,' came back the quick response. 'We all value our independence but it shouldn't be confused with an entitlement to indolence at the expense of those who really do work.'

'George and I both work,' Rose interjected.

'Because you live in the yard at the back of our house and can come to father's workroom, it doesn't mean that you do enough work there to pay your way. Be honest, Rose, you could do better if you went into service.' Hannah was determined to have it out with her sister.

'And who would take a married woman into service?' asked Rose. 'If you took any notice of the Suffragettes, you'd know that they are trying to improve women's rights to work as well as their right to vote.'

'They assume that all women *want* to work,' retorted Hannah. 'Or that they're *capable* of working.'

George was silent throughout this altercation. Unusually, it was John who interjected. 'Look at this,' he said, pointing to a tiny paragraph on the back page of the Gazette. 'Apparently Austria has declared war on Serbia. Perhaps you girls should go to Austria or Serbia! We British have more sense than to go to war with anyone and, in the unlikely event that we did, our brave boys would see them all off in no time. But, if you don't mind, I'd rather read about a ridiculous war in far off country than have my Sundays disrupted by warring females.'

The room fell silent. Sarah looked approvingly at her husband. 'He may not seem to be much of a presence in this town,' she thought, 'but he has a shrewd grasp of affairs.'

◆ ◆ ◆

The moors of Fylingdales shimmered in the hot sun of July 1914, and at Thorney Brow, the hot weather made it hard on those who struggled to bring in the harvest. They thanked the dry days for allowing them to cut the corn, bind it into sheaves and stack it in stooks, but this year their workload was increased as there were problems with livestock. Fowls were moulting, a calving cow had developed milk fever, and one of the horses was lame. Long working days and restless nights created constant exhaustion.

In the farmhouse, Jane and Margaret spent their time catering for the family and for labourers, yet there was a palpable difference in their demeanour this year and they worked with a different rhythm. There was an air of finality about all that they did, and a heightened sense of pride mixed with a tinge of sadness. This was to be their last year at Thorney Brow.

Jane, Margaret, Henry, Gowan and Reginald had met in the big farm kitchen and, for the first time, there had been no argument from Jane when the rest of the assembled company combined their voices to suggest that she should retire. She was eighty-one years old. She, Margaret and Henry would move to Glenean in Hawsker, the cottage she had bought in 1901 when Tamar's death had thwarted her plans to retire. Now, her time had come.

To drag herself away from a lifetime's commitment was hard

for Jane, despite the fact that she had planned her move for so long. But her consolation was that the new custodian of her lifetime's work would be her youngest and favourite son, Gowan. William and his family were secure at Low Flask Farm, and John had no interest in Thorney Brow. It was agreed that Gowan needed better living conditions and that the tragedies that had beset him entitled him to family support. He, Fran and their children, Herbert aged five, Kathleen aged three, and Annie, twenty-one months, would move in as soon as the harvest was over, and Jane, Margaret and Henry would leave.

At Browside Cottage, Fran greeted the news that she was to become mistress of Thorney Brow with a mixture of excitement and apprehension. Compared to Browside's four rooms, Thorney Brow would be hard work and its place as the centre of a substantial farming business was, to her, a daunting prospect. She wondered if she would cope.

Gowan threw back his head and laughed at her reticence. 'My mother rose to t' task and, wi' me by tha' side, tha'll be fine,' he had cheerfully announced. 'And it'll be our chance to bring t' family together. Mine and Tamar's children can join us, and Herbert, Kathleen and Annie'll be part o' a bigger family.' Gowan was delighted but Fran was still unsure, and even more so when she considered the prospect of Tamar's children joining them.

Jane's understanding of the frailties of human nature had stood her in good stead throughout her life. Unlike her flamboyant, confident, energetic son, whose tendency was to throw himself into work as a universal panacea, she was inclined to plan. She liked to resolve problems through negotiation and avoid pitfalls rather than work her way out of them. Once she had decided to retire, she wanted to make the transition as smooth as possible. To this end, she recruited Margaret as partner in a scheme to further her ambition. They were to host a family dinner. This would be a chance for all those involved to have their say, air grievances, offer solutions to problems, and pave the way for a new generation to take over her beloved Thorney Brow.

The traditional Sunday dinner was a ritual dating back as long as any Pickering could remember, and on the Sunday of the proposed family dinner, Jane and Margaret were well prepared. This was to be a dinner for Gowan and the children of his first marriage. Jane sat at the head of the table as Margaret served the first course of Yorkshire pudding and gravy.

'Is tha' looking forad to Hawsker, Henry?' Gowan asked.

'Aye. It'll be easier travelling to Robin Hood's Bay wi' me butchery from there in t' winter. But I'll miss t' horses here,' Henry responded. 'I'll mek sure I'm back for t' hunting season though, if tha'll have me, Gowan?'

'I'll keep thee to that promise,' Gowan chuckled.

'Hast tha' sorted out stabling in Hawsker?' queried Reginald.

'Aye. Not a problem.'

The company fell silent. Jane was the first to speak.

'I think we should drink a glass of ale,' she announced. 'We should drink each other's health and toast the decision to put Thorney Brow in good hands.'

Gowan nodded his assent, and they raised a toast as mugs and tankards were clinked together.

It was young Gowan who raised the subject that was on everyone's mind. 'Is tha' wanting me to move here with thee, Father?' he asked. 'Old Mr Burnett will miss me now that he's on his own, and I've taken a liking to living at Howdale Farm over these past years. I'm not disrespecting you, but I don't want to move here.'

Young Gowan's eyes always twinkled. His face showed his joyous love of life and, despite his twenty years, he still had a boyish air about him. He was the son who lightened every problem, brought fun to the family, loved the land, the horses and his heritage, and gave all around him a sense of well-being. To see concern on his features and hear uncertainty in his voice was a signal for his siblings to voice their thoughts.

'I'll not need to stay here for long, if I need to at all,' said Reginald. 'I've been courting Eliza Beeforth, as tha' all knows, and it'll not be long before we're wed and in a place of our own.'

'I heard tell that tha' has'na' got a new tenant for Browside Cottage when tha' leaves it, Father,' chipped in Ernest. 'If tha' agreed, Reginald and I could use it together.'

'And I need to move to Whitby this year, Father. I told you that a while ago. If I'm to become a fully trained teacher, I need to work in the Whitby schools. I wouldn't like to be making the journey here every day when there are lodgings to be had in the town.' Elizabeth Estill, or 'Betty', as she preferred to be called, looked worried.

Tears filled Ethel's eyes as she joined in. 'I so miss Tamar, Father. You surely wouldn't take her away from the Tyremans after all these years. Since our mother died, they've been mother and father to her, and they've already said that I can join her with them. She's twelve years old now, and can leave school. I'm fifteen and can earn my keep, so I'd be no trouble to the Tyremans. Please, Father, let me go to her.'

Gowan had his tankard in his hand, and his meat was untouched on his plate. He looked horrified, mystified, worried. His plans to unite his family, to be surrounded by his children, to offer a bright, new future to the next generation were falling apart.

These young people who surrounded him were no longer young, malleable children. They were adults, or nearly so. Reginald was twenty-three, Ernest twenty-one, young Gowan twenty, Betty seventeen, Ethel fifteen, and Alfred fourteen. Why had he not seen what was in front of his eyes? They were no longer the babies, toddlers and schoolchildren they'd once been. Had he been so bound up in his own new life that he'd missed them growing into adulthood?

John Clark was not sharing their meal because he had already broken away from the land and moved to Carlin How to the ironworks, where he lodged with his cousin, William and Mary's son, also called Gowan.

Gowan had misjudged his children. He had assumed that the ambition that had been in his mind since the day his first wife, Tamar, had died was the same as theirs. Thorney Brow was, to him, his rationale, his life, but to them it was simply part of a wider world. He felt let down, compromised, alone.

His response was characteristic. 'I'll not have this! I'll not listen to ill-conceived plans and outrageous suggestions! I'll not have my children telling me where their futures lie! I offer an opportunity to you all and tha's turning it down! I'll not listen to this nonsense any longer. Rethink! Rethink!' Gowan slammed his tankard on the table, left his meat untouched, and stormed out of the house.

The family was stunned. Silently, they stared at the untouched food and tried to avoid eye contact. Margaret's hands shook. No-one moved.

It was Jane who broke the silence. 'Now there's a pretty pickle!' she said. 'I think we have some work to do. Margaret, put some potatoes on young Ethel's plate. Reginald, top up poor Henry's tankard, and Ernest, for goodness' sake take some of that cabbage before it goes cold. There's an apple pie waiting to be eaten, and I doubt whether leaving it will do ought to improve that son of mine's temper.'

The atmosphere relaxed. Gradually, a quiet but thoughtful conversation started, but uncharacteristically it was Margaret who instigated it. Until then she had said little. Now, she turned a tearful face to her family and, for the first time, they realised what a blow to her the move to Hawsker would be. She would lose the home she had always known and the love of children now grown into adulthood. She told them she could understand why the Tyremans would not want Tamar to leave them, and why old Joseph Burnett would want young Gowan to stay at Howdale Farm. She understood the dichotomy that the change in stewardship of Thorney Brow created; she saw a new opportunity for Gowan's second family, but a lost way of life for the first one.

The effect of Margaret's quietly spoken words was immediate. Ethel hugged her, Betty promised to visit her as often as her time would allow, and even Reginald joined the general need to show she was appreciated by saying that he and Eliza wanted her to be a part of their lives when they married. Young Gowan joked that she 'couldn't get away from him as easily as she thought', and threatened to visit Hawsker so often that they would have to buy in extra sweetmeats to reward him.

Heat, hunger and isolation eventually forced Gowan to return to Thorney Brow. He had climbed a steep track away from the house up to a high point that gave a view of his beloved land, but suddenly tiredness swept over him. Limbs that he had pushed to the limit bringing in the harvest were aching, his back refused to straighten, and perspiration rolled down his face.

He swept his sleeve across his brow, squinted against the brightness of the sun, and steadied himself by leaning his elbow against a rock face. He felt faint, and hunger gnawed at his belly. The anger that had inspired his flight from Thorney Brow evaporated and his own frailties forced a reconsideration of the reason for his distress. He was forty-eight years old, yet he knew he looked older. He had given his all to his farm and family, yet he knew that the best gift he could give them was the freedom to make their own decisions. He had lost the will to fight with them, and he returned to the house.

A united family greeted Gowan, all agreeing that they wished him, Fran and Herbert, Kathleen and Annie good luck in their new home, but Thorney Brow would not see him reunited under one roof with his other children. Reginald, Ernest and Alfred would live at Browside Cottage; young Gowan would stay at Howdale Farm; Betty would find lodgings in Whitby, and Ethel would join her beloved sister, Tamar, at the blacksmith's forge and cottage with the Tyremans at Thorpe. He could not argue. It had been decided.

That night, Jane Pickering went to bed feeling satisfied. Sunday dinner had provided an opportunity to deal with issues that she knew had been simmering. If left to boil, they could have irrevocably damaged her family's peace of mind and future. She had dreaded leaving Thorney Brow with a family rift. 1914, she decided, would not see a war amongst the Pickerings. It would be a good year, and she could think of nothing now that could damage the prospects of a settled and promising future.

At Browside, Fran felt a wave of relief sweep through her being when she learned of the family's decision. Thorney Brow would be home to her, Gowan and their children alone.

THIRTEEN

'WHAT A DAY to choose!' Lily complained to her mother. 'Fancy having to leave such a wonderful atmosphere to go to the moors!'

'Nonsense, dear. You'll see Fran again, and you'll see little Kathleen and Annie. You'll enjoy the break. Just because Gowan agreed to Herbert living with us when Fran needed help, he'd not be too happy if we didn't make sure the boy went home for the holidays. Anyway, moving to Thorney Brow and having two more little ones to cope with has been hard for her, but Fran'll want to see her son. And she'll want to see you!'

'I do understand, Mother, but you have to admit Whitby's a bit special at the moment.'

It was August 1914. Britain had declared war on Germany and the townspeople of Whitby greeted the news with enthusiasm, convinced that Britain would soon teach the Hun a lesson. The Mission to Seamen was festooned with bunting. Union flags hung from commercial premises on Church Street, alongside the harbour, outside the spa and even in Flowergate. Bands played and young men strutted in their new uniforms. Outside the Drill Hall, a sergeant from the Princess of Wales Yorkshire Hussars loudly proclaimed the worth of those who were enlisting. The queue of recruits was flanked by relatives proud to see their nearest and dearest doing their bit for king and country. The whole town had a party atmosphere.

At Thorney Brow, Fran was excited. She was going to see her favourite sister and her son, and she'd be able to show off her new home. When they arrived, Herbert was eager to tell his mother stories of bands and marching soldiers and about his friends at Cliff Street School. Kathleen wanted to tell her Aunt Lily about the horses she loved, and chubby little Annie shyly peeped at the newcomers. The kitchen was spacious, and the atmosphere relaxed.

'Perhaps,' Lily thought, 'life here on the moors is not as bad as I envisaged. And Thorney Brow is an impressive place.'

Gowan came in from the farm to join them. He chucked Herbert under his chin with a brief, 'Time you were back, young man. There's work for you to do here,' and greeted Lily with, 'Hello, Lily. My little wife's been looking forward to tha' visit. Are you and t' rest of t' family well?'

'I'm well, thank you, Gowan. The family sends their kindest regards. I hope your new life here is suiting you.'

'It suits me well. I love this place, Lily, and I think tha' sister'll grow to love it too in time.' He turned to Fran and said with a broad smile, 'You're learning, aren't you, little wife?'

Fran looked embarrassed. 'I think I've got a long way to go to compete with your mother, Gowan. I'm not sure I'll ever be as proficient as her. But I'll do my best.'

Gowan looked pleased. He was about to return to the stable but, as he turned to pull the kitchen door behind him, he paused and remarked, 'I'll take Kathleen back wi' me, Fran. You know how much she loves the horses. It's a pity young Herbert is na' as good wi' t' animals as she is. I think you've got some work to do on that young man.'

Smiling, he said jokingly to Lily, 'I'll have to rely on you, Lily, to persuade that sister of yours to stop treating Herbert like a girl whenever she sees him! He'd make a fine farmer if he was given more encouragement to work in the fields.' With Kathleen happily in tow but leaving Herbert on the verge of tears, Gowan left.

Lily said nothing. Her opinion of Gowan had never been good; to her, he was treating his wife like a child, undermining her authority with the children, and expecting her to become a copy of his mother. But she bit her tongue.

'Come with me, Lily. I'll show you round the house,' said Fran.

Lily was impressed with the house, despite her underlying prejudices. All the rooms were substantial, and all gave a feeling of permanence. Huge beams supported the ceilings, solid plank doors fastened with heavy latches separated the rooms, and heavy, square flagstones showing the wear and tear of generations graced the ground floor.

The kitchen was definitely lacking. There was no running water, and cooking on the huge range meant lighting a fire which was oppressively hot in summer. The pantry and dairy faced north and were comparatively cool but they bore witness to the effort required to feed the family. In the pantry, Kilner jars contained jams, pickles and preserves, and there were sacks of potatoes, onions, carrots, swede and turnip, whilst in the dairy there were cheeses, hams, butter and eggs.

The privy at the rear of the house was little more than a roughly constructed shed covering an open drain, and Lily found it quite offensive, especially as the weather was warm. But the parlour was a delight. Its huge, panelled inglenook was big enough to accommodate two substantial settles, and the oak chairs elsewhere in the room were both serviceable and imposing. Although not to her taste, the walls were adorned with paintings in heavy gilt frames depicting prize rams, pigs and, most prominently, horses. A heavy wool rug lay in front of the fire; Lily remarked that their mother would have an apoplexy if she were with them for a large dog was sleeping peacefully on it. They laughed and Fran agreed that Sarah Booth's idea of luxury and good taste was probably very much at odds with Pickering opinions.

Their tour finished upstairs, where Fran was anxious to let Lily see her and Gowan's bedroom. 'Quick, Lily, do have a look,' she said, and ushered Lily into what appeared to be a vast and impressive space.

Wide oak planks littered with a motley selection of rugs made the room inviting and, like the parlour below, the walls were panelled in dark oak, but there the similarity ended. A big four-poster bed dominated, whilst on either side of the door were wardrobes that appeared to be constructed of ancient, seasoned oak. A deep armchair stood to one side of the window. Heavy curtains were drawn back, revealing a magnificent view of the farmyard, outbuildings and the moors beyond. This was an opulent room, very much the room of the master of the house.

'Let me see the children's rooms,' Lily asked.

The contrast was stark.

'Children need food, clothing and healthy living. Gowan says they don't appreciate fine furniture or ornamentation. I know Kathleen would rather have a puppy than a fine chair, and Annie loves her doll.'

'And Herbert?'

'Oh, you know he's happy so long as he has a book to read!'

'So rooms with only the basic necessities are sufficient for children, are they? A bed, a chest of drawers to share, if necessary, and nothing more?'

'Gowan says it's enough.'

At the end of their tour, Lily retired to her room to unpack the few items she had brought with her. Herbert was in the kitchen with Annie and she was glad to be alone. She needed to collect her thoughts. Was she over-sensitive? There seemed to be no sign from Fran that anything was lacking from her new home but, despite the structure being fine, the facilities were basic and the children's rooms were almost bare. 'Gowan says' seemed to be Fran's new rationale.

Was Fran happy to be treated in such a way? Certainly, she'd heard no word of complaint. In fact, precisely the opposite. She seemed to hang on the man's every word. And what about the children? Kathleen was happy enough – a 'chip off the old block'. Annie was too young to be aware of anything other than her precious doll. But what of Herbert? The child had little chance of pleasing his father unless he suddenly became more like his sister, and she knew that the little boy's time at Flowergate was contributing to his preference for books rather than farm life.

'I really must try to put my prejudices aside,' Lily decided eventually. 'It is not for me to judge the worth of a marriage or the happiness of others. Fran's clothes are coarse, antiquated and peasant-like, and she looks tired. Her hands are rough and her demeanour is lacklustre despite her apparent pleasure at seeing me, but she has only just begun her new life here. She needs time to adjust. Perhaps soon, an attempt will be made to modernise this place and make life easier for her.' She couldn't resist a sarcastic aside to herself, 'If Gowan says...!'

By the time Lily returned to the kitchen to help Fran with the evening meal, she was calm and relatively relaxed. But when her sister remarked that the new fashion for showing a woman's ankles suited Lily, she suggested that they make one for Fran in the same style. 'We're not our father's daughters if we can't make a skirt!'

To her surprise, the suggestion was greeted with immediate resistance. 'I'm sorry, Fran. I didn't mean to offend you, I just thought you might like a new outfit.'

'Oh, Lily! You silly girl! It's got nothing to do with me not wanting a new outfit, though I don't know that I would ever have occasion to wear it. It's simply the practicalities of fitting it. I have not yet told you my news. It's too early for you to have suspected, but now that you've put me on the spot, I must tell you. I am expecting another child!'

Lily was taken aback. This would be Fran's fourth baby. For once, Gowan was right: the clothes that his wife wore were perfectly suited to the purpose. Modern dresses and skirts that accentuated the shape of a woman's body were unlikely to appeal at Thorney Brow. And, at this rate, basic bedrooms for children were probably the only way to live.

'You look really surprised, Lily.' Fran broke her sister's train of thought. 'Are you not going to congratulate me?'

Lily jerked her mind back to the present. 'I'm sorry, Fran. Of course I congratulate you.' She hugged her sister and, remembering her manners, asked, 'Are you feeling well? Is the pregnancy progressing as it should?'

'I think so.'

'Well, the Pickerings seem intent on populating the world!' Lily remarked wryly.

Fran laughed. 'It seems to be a bit of a Pickering tradition, Lily! Gowan's brother, William, and his wife, Mary, have twelve children, and Mary seems to do very well.'

'That's providing she never wants to leave the farm and is happy spending her life catering for a family with no opportunity to do a single thing for herself!' retorted Lily. She immediately regretted her outburst when Fran looked upset.

Lily decided that keeping her counsel was going to be more difficult than she had imagined. She was quiet for the rest of the evening, retiring to bed on the pretext that the journey had tired her. She slept badly as her mind dwelt on the loss of the attractive, lively and imaginative sister she had once known.

The following morning, Lily was in the kitchen chatting to the children.

'Father says I'll be an excellent horsewoman, and I'm not afraid of them. I even like pigs. They're such funny creatures. I'm not like Herbert and Annie, you know. They don't like the farm animals,' Kathleen announced. 'You hate the animals, don't you, Annie? You're frightened. But I'll look after you. Father says I'm a good second mother to you, and you are my best friend, aren't you?'

Annie beamed with pleasure and stood close to her sister whom she idolised.

'Shall we gather some bilberries today? I saw some growing not far from here when Herbert and I walked from the station,' suggested Lily.

The children looked delighted, but Fran was less sure. 'Oh, Lily, that would be lovely for the girls, but Gowan and I talked after you went to bed last night, and he thinks Herbert should make up for the time he's away from the farm. I don't think he'd be happy at the boy joining you. Herbert has work to do.'

Herbert looked horrified and pleaded with his mother, but Fran was adamant and reminded him how unpleasant it could be to upset his father. Herbert assumed a resigned expression and agreed; he had no desire to see his father in a rage.

Turning to Lily, Fran apologised. 'Summer is a time of heavy manual work in the fields, Lily. Herbert is nearly six years old and perfectly old enough to be of use.' She looked quizzically at Lily's dress. 'I don't think that dress will survive foraging for bilberries. Would you like to borrow one of my aprons?'

Lily had to accept defeat. Donning a voluminous apron that was more like a smock, she groaned inwardly. She felt very similar to the peasant-like individual she had criticised her sister for becoming, but resigned herself to the practicalities of life on the moors. She and the girls set off.

As they neared the outbuildings, they heard the sound of heavy manual work – beating, sweeping and the crash of wood and metal – coming from where Gowan, Reginald and young Gowan were threshing. As soon as they were in sight, the men stopped to wave.

Young Gowan broke free from the group and ran to greet

them. Sweat was pouring down his face and he looked exhausted, but he seemed eager to talk to Lily. 'Hello, Miss Booth,' he panted breathlessly. 'It's good to see you. I so wanted to talk to you.'

'Really?' Lily was surprised.

'Yes, I want to know what Whitby is like at present and what you know of the recruitment. Father says I can enlist as soon as the threshing's over. My cousins Will and Henry, William and Mary's lads, are going to join up alongside me. Do you think the war will be over by then, Miss Booth? Everyone says it'll be over by Christmas, and we don't want to miss the show.'

'Oh my! I don't think you've much to worry about!' she answered with a smile. 'They're still keen to recruit young fellows like you.' Lily described the scenes she had left only the day before and Gowan's eyes glowed with excitement.

He shouted to his father and brother, 'Come and hear what it's like in Whitby. I can't wait to be part of it.'

Gowan joined his son. 'These young bucks'll walk all over the Hun, but I doubt they'll be finished this side o' Christmas. You know, Miss Booth, they say that in some parts of t' country, farmers get twice t' grain from their fields that we do, and they get twice t' yields of milk from their cows. 'Tis hard farming poor soil such as this, but there's profit to be made from wars and there's a chance that a few months o' fighting'll pay for a threshing machine. I'm too old for t' military, but I'm not too old to profit from my land. Reginald has no taste for a uniform, but he agrees with me. We'll possibly see the end of back-breaking work such as we're doing now and that'll be no bad thing.'

'So you're happy to see your son risk his life for a longer time so that you can benefit from the price of corn?' queried Lily.

'Nonsense, woman! There's no fear of the boys getting hurt – it's not the Hun that's the problem. It's those toffs in high places. Kitchener'll knock our boys into shape, but t' rest of them couldn't organise a bairn's tea party. It'll be over by the time they've got the show on the road, but they're so disorganised they'll not bring the boys back home as fast as people think. T' Army and the Navy and everyone else has to eat, haven't they? Mark my words, there'll be a profit in this. Am I not right in saying that there was a shortage of bread and cake in Whitby over the Bank Holiday?

Lily had to admit he was right.

'There you are, shortages of flour already! This war looks promising to me.' Gowan bade her goodbye and he and his son returned to the threshing floor whilst she and the girls continued their quest to find bilberries.

At Thorney Brow, Gowan had told Herbert to clean out the pigsties, and the boy reluctantly began shovelling piles of muck. When the men stopped for a break, Herbert joined them.

Later, Gowan returned to the sties. 'Where are tha', Herbert?' he called cheerfully.

Herbert had finished his work and heard a sound coming from one of the outbuildings. His curiosity had got the better of him and he'd gone to explore. There, curled up on some discarded sacking, was a cat nursing her kittens. He was fascinated. Carefully and gently, he'd lifted each kitten and inspected it. There were five: three black and white, one almost pure black, and a fifth – in his opinion, the prettiest – was tortoiseshell. Each was a mewling, fluffy ball of fur.

His father found him. 'Right, lad! Mek' tha'self useful. Go to t' keld and fetch a bucket of water.' Herbert did as he was told. 'Now, put that bit o' vermin in t' bucket and drown it.'

Herbert looked horrified. 'I can't do that, Father! They're so pretty. And I've been watching the mother cat. She's so careful with them. I can't kill her babies.'

'Tha'll do as tha's told, lad. We don't work the way we work to support a load o' feral cats. T' damned vermin breed like rabbits.

143

Get t' job done.'

Herbert stood rooted to the spot, clutching the kitten. Suddenly, he dropped the little creature, burst into tears and turned to run to the house. Gowan's reactions were quick; grabbing an old riding crop he had used earlier to guide the pigs into the field, he struck the boy hard.

Herbert's next memories were of a sharp pain in his back, a feeling of sickness and of landing on the ground with a thud. Sobbing and dazed, he stumbled into the kitchen minutes before Lily and the girls returned from their outing.

The girls' lively chatter ceased. Lily went to her sister, who was comforting Herbert, and asked him to explain. Before he could attempt an answer, Gowan arrived. 'You can stop mollycoddling that boy,' he shouted. 'He'll learn to do as he's told. You can take some of the blame for this, Lily, you and that family of yours. Herbert needs discipline and somebody's got to start making a man of him.'

He turned to Fran. 'Come on, Fran. Help me knock that young fellow into shape. Just ignore his baby howls. He'll live! He can work if he puts his mind to it – he's proved it today. Anyway, he's only being trained in the same way I've trained all my children. Mark my words, one day he'll look up to me and be glad that he has such a fine inheritance. His back will heal, but his respect for his father will grow.'

Lily said nothing. Later, after she had eaten a meal she did not enjoy, during which Gowan remarked on her silence, she kissed the children goodbye and ran her hand across Herbert's back. She could feel the weals where a blow had left its mark.

She was dreading her journey home, for Gowan had been insistent that he take her to the station where he had some business to attend to. The journey was a fraught one. At first, Lily sat in silence, but Gowan would have none of it. 'Come on, Lily. Tell me what an evil father I am, and tell me that in the town a load of feral cats would be allowed to live off food that would be better eaten by hungry children.'

Lily shuddered but felt her anger rise. She retorted, 'No, Gowan, I am not suggesting that feral cats should be tolerated. My own father has had the unpleasant job of drowning kittens occasionally. But I think a five-year-old boy should not be beaten for refusing the task.'

'So a five-year-old boy should disobey his father, then?'

'No! His father should not ask so much of him.'

'I ask my children to do as they're told, and I ask no more of 'em than they can do. There's far too much emphasis put on t' so called rights of children these days, Lily. I blame t' present government for a lot of it. I might admire Asquith for his tenacity, and I'm proud of his Yorkshire heritage, but his Liberal policies are hard to stomach. The so called "Children's Charter" was intended to help the poorest children, but it seems to involve questioning the nation's attitude to what a man can do in his own home. In my eyes, an Englishman's home is his castle and I'll thank liberal-minded folk – and that includes you, Lily – no matter how well intentioned, to keep their noses out of my business. I am a well-respected man in these parts, and I doubt anyone around here would agree with you if you suggested that I needed guidance on how to treat my family. Go home to nurse your prejudices and live your smug, middle-class life, but don't try to impose your ways on me.'

Lily decided not to give him the satisfaction of knowing he had upset her. She made no reply but simply gazed at the moors, the woods and, in the distance, the sea. Usually, the landscape gave her pleasure. Today, it gave none. She questioned herself.

It was true, the Pickerings were well-respected. They farmed vast acres of land, were pillars of the church, and successful in business. Her nonconformist and liberal-minded ideas were based on an assumption that society had a duty to care for the most vulnerable; that had been interpreted as the sick, the poor and families who, for whatever reason, could not care for their own – not a family such as the one her sister had married into.

Could it be that cruelty existed in every level of society? Could the more articulate excuse their behaviour so effectively that they went unpunished for their excesses, whilst those on the lowest rung of the social ladder were castigated for the same crimes? Certainly, men like Gowan Pickering could be very persuasive for they exuded confidence. But what about her sister? Was she not complicit in the actions of her husband?

Lily felt she had lost the sister she had once known; now she questioned whether she had ever known Fran at all. Had she merely assumed that a teacher would be a good mother, and that a girl who delighted in the arts, appreciated beauty, and had a sensitive nature would apply that sensitivity to the up-bringing of her children? Was Fran so infatuated with Gowan that she failed to see beneath the charismatic, flamboyant exterior, the claims to power and the flaunted ambition? Or could it be that women had no choice? They had few rights, were totally dependent on their husbands and, on the wild moors of Fylingdales, could not expect the support of neighbours and friends in the same way as a woman who lived in the town.

In Fran's case, her neighbours and friends – if she had any – were Gowan's family.

FOURTEEN

'THOSE POOR LADS!' Jane Pickering sat in the parlour of Glenean gazing across the land adjoining her house, and contemplated the difficulties that a combination of weather and war had inflicted on her sons. A vase containing carefully arranged blackthorn twigs with buds about to erupt into delicate white blossom was, to her, a portent of better days to come, but a copy of the *Whitby Gazette* had dampened her spirits with an advertisement for 'Shoeing Smiths'.

'There'll be no skills left in t' countryside at this rate!' she murmured. 'Five shillings a day t' army's offering. No farmer could afford to pay a smith enough to mek that sort of money. And t' army still wants more men, so long as they're over five foot and an inch in height. Is this government determined to ruin us? I thought those clever people in London said t' war would be over by Christmas and it's nearly Easter!'

Margaret brought her a cup of tea, the universal panacea for all woes, and commiserated. 'Now then, Mother, Gowan'll cope. He always does!'

No-one had thought that Jane would settle easily to a life away from Thorney Brow but she proved them wrong, as she had done so often before. For Margaret, the house was a relief. For the first time since her marriage, she could concentrate her energies on caring for a home, choose furnishings and fabrics, and enjoy the company of her wider family without having to feed or care for them.

Both Jane and Margaret were proud of their new home.

147

Glenean stood at the very edge of High Hawsker, with views across open fields to the front, rear and side. Detached from its neighbours, its slight elevation, imposing cream brickwork, sash windows, and centrally positioned front door surmounted by a delicately moulded fanlight gave it individuality. It was not ostentatious but different from the stone structures of the rest of the village.

Jane's concern for her sons' welfare was the result of a visit from Gowan. He had called to see her on his way back from Whitby, where he'd negotiated prices for market produce and ordered timber he needed for repairs. He'd caught the train from Whitby but, instead of continuing his journey home to the moors, he'd stopped off at Hawsker.

Jane looked forward to his visits. She never knew when he was likely to turn up but she knew he would, for the bond between mother and son was strong. She had greeted him with her customary, 'Good to see thee, lad.' Calling to Margaret, she added, 'Put t' kettle on, lass. Tha' brother's in need of a brew.'

Gowan was cold, tired and, in Jane's opinion, needing some rest and a little cosseting, especially now that the number of labourers on the land was depleted by young men joining up – including five of her grandchildren.

'They'll all mek fine additions to our forces,' Jane remarked. 'But they can't be replaced by just anyone. I've heard t' government thinks that townsfolk could work the land, or even women but, that's typical of t' men in suits and bowler hats!'

Gowan chatted to his mother about his visit to Whitby. They agreed that moorland farmers were seldom treated with the respect they deserved, and that the government's new initiatives to try to ensure fair prices for their goods were a complete waste of time. Individuals like Gowan were perfectly capable of negotiating their own prices.

'Eighty-two years old!' he thought. 'And still alert to the goings on of the world and her family. But it's as well she can put her feet up. Living at Glenean will be so much better for her and for Margaret. No need to fetch water from t' well because there's a village pump, and no need to worry about livestock, for Henry's a good man and will supply them with meat and mek sure they've got oil and wicks for t' lamps.'

Gowan was not looking forward to going home. Fran's pregnancy had not gone well and, as a temporary measure, he had agreed to Kathleen joining her brother, Herbert, in Whitby and enrolling at Cliff Street School. Unlike her brother, Kathleen had not wanted to go. She had cried and Gowan had found himself in the invidious position of being beholden to his in-laws whilst empathising with his daughter who, like him, did not thrive in the claustrophobic atmosphere of the town. And he'd had to pay for the privilege! He had to compensate the Booth family for taking in two young children, feeding and caring for them, because they took up space that could be rented out .

Despite that, he knew the decision had been the right one. There were now two fewer mouths to feed at Thorney Brow, where even caring for the amenable little Annie had proved difficult for his wife. Now Fran was in the late stages of pregnancy, her mother had come to help and the prospect of dealing with Sarah Booth did nothing to raise his spirits.

Financially, the war was doing Gowan proud because prices for basic foodstuffs had risen. He had looked at the motor charabanc that an acquaintance, Tommy Craggs, had bought and was intending to use for paying passengers to travel from the Flask Inn to Whitby.

'If young Tommy can look at a chara, then I'll set my sights on both a threshing machine and possibly a motor lorry if t' war goes on for a while longer. 'Tis an ill wind that blows nobody any good,' he thought.

But Gowan knew that profits depended on produce, and hiring labour for the farm had caused severe difficulties. Unusually, neither the Pickering brothers nor their neighbours had been able to share their burdens, as they all faced the same problem. He counted himself lucky that he had his older sons to help, but he had been forced to employ some itinerant workers whose presence he resented and whose services he used as little as he could.

Fran and Sarah were enjoying each other's company at Thorney Brow. For Lent, Fran had produced traditional pancakes and cut down on some of the more extravagant foods such as cake, but the Pickerings had a knack of avoiding the harshest of church dictates. The meal that she and her mother prepared for the family that evening paid only lip-service to the fasting season.

They were preoccupied with the likelihood of the new baby arriving before Easter. Fran was convinced that it would, but wished the weather were more predictable because Dr Ross was in Robin Hood's Bay. Although she felt it highly unlikely that his services would be called on, she said she would feel happier if she knew the road was passable.

When Gowan returned, the atmosphere was convivial. Conversation revolved around the presence of sailors in Whitby, the extortionate price of some of the food in the shops, the terrible time when a German frigate had accidentally landed a shot on Whitby Abbey, and pleasantries about old Jane Pickering's health and her surprisingly rapid adaptation to life in Hawsker.

It wasn't until Sarah remarked that Lily had expressed a fancy to join them for a day or two that the atmosphere grew tense. 'I'm sure you'd have little objection to her coming, would you, dear?' she asked Gowan.

'None at all,' came the surprising response. 'I doubt I'll see much of her, for I canna' be of real help when it comes to babies

150

arriving, and there's burnin' to be done on t' moors.'

'What do you mean, there's burning to be done?' Sarah asked. 'What if you're needed to fetch Dr Ross?'

'Fran'll not have need of a doctor, woman! She's a Pickering now! And, as for t' burnin' – you know full well that t' moors need a good burnin' off in spring. Wi'out it, t' gorse and shrubs and even birch would tek root and there'd be no grazing for t' sheep or cover for t' grouse. T' weather might have thrown t' odd blizzard at us, but it's bin' dry for t' last few days so we need to tek advantage while we can.'

'But, Gowan, there's a war on! You can't let the light from blazing fires on the moors act as a guide for the Germans! The glow will be seen well after dark, for the fires do not die down in an instant. Think of our poor boys risking their lives to fight, and being hindered by the likes of you putting out the equivalent of beacons! In Whitby, everyone is being cautious about showing lights at night, and the constable is very vigilant.'

'So you'd rather t' nation starved to death, would you? Where are t' sheep supposed to graze if the moors become unusable? Tha's no concept of farming! I'll not be troubling you by telling you how to run a home and family, and I'd be grateful if you'd oblige me in the same way by keeping your nose out of my affairs.'

The next day, Gowan set off for the moors and Lily arrived from Whitby. She was needed for the chapel services on Sundays and taught music throughout the week, but she'd managed to make time to see for herself that her sister was well. Despite her usual reticence when it came to offering praise for life on the moors, she had to admit that she was looking forward to her break.

As she walked from the station, she was glad of the contrast to town life. Whitby had lost some of its vibrancy as the troops arrived, youngsters left and holidaymakers stayed away. Only that morning, the station had bustled with the arrival of a battalion of army cyclists who were drafted in for accommodation in the empty boarding houses. Even her parents' home had been checked by the military authorities as a possible destination.

Lily had been preoccupied recently with the welfare of a man she had come to realise was very important to her. She had met Herbert Watson at the Mission to Seamen. She had told her mother about him – and Sarah had not been impressed.

'Are my daughters intent on ruining their lives?' she complained. 'One marries a good for nothing so-called carpenter and joiner, another marries a self-opinionated bully and resigns herself to deprivation on the moors and a third wants to marry a Jack Tar who'll either drown, get killed or be maimed. And even if that doesn't happen, he will never be around to give the support she'll need.'

Reluctantly Sarah had agreed to Lily inviting Bert to tea, and had agreed that he was a nice young man. But Lily had heard nothing of him since that day; now, as she walked from the station to Thorney Brow, she was preoccupied with thoughts of Bert's whereabouts and safety.

She stopped as she caught her first glimpse of the moors, and her mind switched from introspection to anger. In contrast to the clear skies to the east, clouds of dark smoke were rising up from the earth. Lily was horrified. 'They're surely not burning the moors at a time like this!' she muttered to herself.

As soon as she arrived at Thorney Brow, Fran and her mother assured her that yes, the moors were being burned.

Gowan had ridden his horse to Low Flask Farm where his brother, William joined him. Together they walked out to the open ground where men and boys were congregating. The Pickerings and their neighbours decided exactly which parts of the moor they would target.

Dogs were sent to chase away stray sheep grazing in places

where they would be in danger, and a variety of tools ranging from tree branches to wooden-shafted paddles were prepared to control the fire.

A shout went up, faggots were lit, and gradually tiny flames created smoky clumps that blazed into fierce, crackling fires. The tranquil moorland scene came alive: grouse flew, dogs barked, sheep fled, and the air filled with dark, acrid smoke. Flames leapt high above the men's heads, sparks danced in the air and a pall of black-grey smoke blotted out the rays of the weak spring sun.

As the heat became intense, muscles tightened; the men were afraid they would lose control of the conflagration. Slowly rich, black, sooty embers replaced the bracken, heather and gorse. The men defined the course of the fire by beating the earth around the area. They perspired, their eyes streamed and they coughed. Periodically, someone would run to the murky water nearby to quench his thirst or, if he had been unlucky, splash water on a limb, hand or face that had been caught by a spark.

The task was exhausting, tense and unrelenting. No-one dared leave the flames or lose concentration. Gowan was in his element. Just as a horse galloping across open ground, or a fox racing to escape his dogs, or a hare avoiding capture made his pulse race, a moorland fire excited and energised him. It offered hard, physical effort and the camaraderie of others. His commanding voice, tall, athletic figure and familiarity with the moors gave him status, and he revelled in it. He did what he always did and pushed himself to the limit, refusing to stop for a break, refusing more than a mouthful of peaty water, fiercely determined that as much of the moor as possible would be controlled and burned by the assembled company.

At the end of the day when the fires died down and black, scorched earth scarred the landscape, boys were left to guard against the chance of wind fanning the embers back to life. Gowan, William and the rest of the men adjourned to the Flask

Inn. Faces blackened, eyes bloodshot, hair streaked with perspiration and the debris of burnt furze, they quenched their thirst with cold beer.

They laughed at the antics of some of the new arrivals on the moors who had sought work when farmers' sons had gone to war but had no idea how to deal with moorland life. Now, they could boast scars from burns and charred clothing, even claim damaged boots as souvenirs, as they congratulated themselves on a job well done.

As daylight faded and shadows played in the hedgerows, they headed home to eat and rest, safe in the knowledge that their families had tended their cattle, pigs, chickens and homes during their absence, and that their own endeavours had secured the use of the moors for another year.

Gowan arrived back at Thorney Brow to find the children asleep and the labourers in their accommodation in the outhouse, which they shared with overwintering cattle and lambing ewes. Fran, Sarah and Lily were in the parlour. A meal was waiting for him in the kitchen.

He rinsed his hands in the water that flowed from the high ground at the front of the house and greeted Fran with a curt, 'Now then, lass,' as she left her mother and sister and joined him in the kitchen. As she placed a plate of food in front of him, tiredness overwhelmed him. He unlaced his boots, threw his jacket on a chair and sat at the table with his elbows propping up his head. He spooned food into his mouth, drank a mug of steaming tea, then yawned and stretched.

Lily came into the kitchen. 'Had a good day, Gowan?' she asked.

'Tiring, but we got t' job done,' he answered.

Sarah joined them. Her face reflected her thoughts; her brow was furrowed and her jawline set. 'I think you finished your work at the Flask!' she remarked. 'I can always tell if a man's been drinking.'

'And I presume that's a problem to you, is it?' Gowan retorted and made to leave the room.

'Only when it involves leaving your pregnant wife and the work that needs doing here on the farm!' came the quick reply.

Lily joined in. 'I'm sorry, Gowan, but I must speak my mind. The glow of the moorland fires lights up the sky and puts the lives of our brave sailors at risk by lighting up targets for the enemy. You seem determined to behave as if there were no war.'

'And as if you had no responsibilities at home!' Sarah added. 'Do your realise, your wife could go into labour at any time? Just look at her. Surely you should be here and not at the inn! I can't believe you left her and couldn't even be bothered to join us for a meal.'

There was a deafening silence in the room. Fran looked embarrassed. Gowan glowered at his mother-in-law and Lily. Suddenly he pulled his weary body erect and straightened his back. His commanding voice boomed across the room.

'Lily,' he said, 'I can understand your fear for tha's taken up wi' a sailor. But you!' He turned to Sarah. 'This is my home, my farm, my family. And I think, in view of your insistence that you know my business better 'n I do, it'd be better if you returned to Whitby. Maybe there, your words of wisdom and profound understanding of everything you encounter'll be appreciated. Pack your bags. It is too late to catch t' train tonight, but I want you gone tomorrow. You're trouble. You and your kind'll never understand t' ways of t' moors. I'm tired and I don't need this aggravation. I work hard. I provide for my family. I don't need you, Fran doesn't need you. Go, woman! Go!'

Having vented his anger, Gowan slammed the door behind him and loudly made his way upstairs to bed. Fran stood rigidly next to the stove where she had gone to replenish the teapot. Lily gazed at her mother in awe. Sarah looked nonplussed as she fidgeted with the sleeve on her dress.

'Mother, I think you have pushed Gowan too far,' Lily said quietly. 'I know you always act in what you think are the best interests of your family, but it looks as if your words this time have been counterproductive. You've done nothing but anger the man. Unless you can placate him somehow in the morning, I think you have no choice but to leave.'

Sarah appeared to be in a state of shock. For a moment she made no response, but then she turned to Fran and voiced the thoughts that had been in both her and Lily's minds for a long time. 'Fran,' she said, 'regardless of whether or not I have spoken out of turn, I think Gowan's outbursts are unreasonable and his angry moods a source of concern. This is not the first time I have witnessed them. He never accepts discussion as a way of communication. He constantly quotes the old adage "actions speak louder than words", but he seems to prefer that either no words are used or the only ones to be heard are his. He always has to be right. How do you put up with it? How can you support a man who dominates you, frightens both you and your children, has no respect for any of us and seems to think he is a law unto himself? Is there nothing you can do to control him? Has he no regard for your feelings? Does he beat you in the same way as he beats his children? Does he bully you? I suspect he does. Or are you so malleable that you are like putty in his hands and obey his every command? It looks as if you have no say in what happens in your own home, and I suspect that the longer he's allowed to get away with this behaviour, the less likely he is to change. Do you have nothing to say?'

Fran hesitated. Her distress was evident, but she appeared to be considering the words she wanted to use carefully. She sat down and gazed at her fingernails. At last, she gave her response.

'I love you, Mother, and I love you too, Lily, but neither of you has ever accepted that I also love Gowan.' She paused then continued. 'The rugged landscape that drew me when I first encountered it batters the senses with its wild magnificence and its emptiness, but I should have realised that it provides a hard living for those who seek to tame it. Gowan must bring up his children to face the hardships it will inflict on them and simultaneously provide bread and meat for his family.

'Instead of criticising him, you should criticise me. The pretty pictures I had of acres of moorland, glistening seas, towering cliffs and huntsmen racing across the landscape were fanciful and romantic. Gowan has taught me that farming in this part of the world is hard. It requires energy, strength and stamina, qualities that he has. He is older than me, and wiser. He has accepted that I am a lesser woman than his mother but he has taught me to become part of the farming community. He has taught me to respect the power of nature. He says he has recently begun to have more faith in my abilities and even entrusts me with the care of Thorney Brow.

'A woman must accept her husband's decisions, accept his ways, for there is no alternative. What can I do to change the life I chose to live? How can I change a man who is viewed as a pillar of the local community, the apple of his mother's eye, the successful son, brother and husband? I made my vow, to love, cherish and obey. Please do not ask me to break it. I will obey my husband.

'And please, Mother, I beg you, apologise to Gowan. Accept him. Recognise his anger for what it is, simply frustration with situations that are a source of tension, or outside his compass, or even the result of exhaustion because he works so hard. If he strikes me or my children, it is only because he cares for his land and cares for us. We will learn to be better people for it.'

Sarah and Lily listened in stony silence. Lily was the first to speak. 'Oh, Fran. You are so brainwashed and downtrodden, you appear to have lost your sense of self-worth. Where is the lively, spirited girl we once knew? Where are your womanly wiles? Have you not seen the clever way that Mother manages Father? Could you not do the same with Gowan?'

'I think you have not understood what I've said, Lily,' came the immediate reply. 'Gowan is not Father. He would never take a woman's advice. He is not the malleable soul that our dear father is. And you know he would not accept my opinion when it comes to life on the moors for I am a town-born girl.

'I think both you and Mother speak without thinking. Instead of constantly decrying the way I live my life, I wish you would offer more constructive solutions to the problems you seem intent on finding. Look at the benefits that my life has given me. I have the privilege of living in a beautiful part of the world and a more than adequate roof over my head. My children are fed and, if I have to pull my weight with farm work, I know that it is for my and my children's benefit. If I have to pay for that with the occasional outburst from my husband, so be it.'

The conversation ended, and Sarah and Lily made their way up to bed. Fran joined Gowan, whose loud snoring indicated that tiredness had a greater impact on him than the words he had spoken.

'Perhaps he will forget the disagreement with my mother,' Fran thought. Yet secretly she knew that was unlikely and she dreaded the next day.

FIFTEEN

POCKETS OF EARLY morning mist swirled across the moors and collected in the bracken strewn hollows of the undulating landscape. It collected in bays and rocky outcrops that fringed the sea. The raucous screams of gulls and the early morning chatter of sparrows intermingled in a rhapsody of welcome for the new day, whilst young sheep and calving cattle voiced their resentment at being confined to winter quarters. Itinerant workers emerged from ill-assorted outbuildings to splash cold water from streams onto their faces and shiver at the cold air of dawn, hoping their employers would offer welcome slices of bread, bowls of porridge and cups of hot, sweet tea. Gradually, the moors awoke.

Inside the kitchen of Thorney Brow farmhouse, Fran struggled to coax the burning embers of the fire back to life and collect the requirements of breakfast. She had slept badly. The confrontation with her mother and sister had been exhausting and upsetting. The prospect of Gowan insisting that her mother should return to Whitby daunted her, for a mild ache in her back and a feeling of nausea implied that her baby would shortly make its entrance into the world. She had hoped that Sarah would be by her side; now she felt alone and fragile.

Gowan had slept well and shown no indication that there was anything amiss. If she hadn't known him better, she might have thought that the previous evening had been forgotten. Herbert, Kathleen and Annie joined her and were immediately followed by a worried looking Sarah and a weary, withdrawn Lily.

Two itinerant labourers joined the family in the kitchen for breakfast. The children's chatter made a welcome diversion because it prevented a discussion of a subject that was obviously in the minds of the family.

It was only when Kathleen, her doting sister, and a reluctant Herbert had departed to the farmyard that the three women could have a brief conversation. Sarah and Lily had agreed; they suggested that, rather than risk further confrontation with Gowan, Sarah would return to Whitby but Lily would stay with her sister. She would let her mother apologise to those who would be inconvenienced by her absence from the next Sunday services and the cancellation of lessons.

Fran was unsure. Lily had no experience of childbirth; she was a single woman who had never shown any interest in anything relating to women's health issues, and had virtually no knowledge of farming. Fran had considered her mother to be out of place in a rural environment, but Lily was even more inept. Yet a compromise was needed and this was probably the best that could be found.

Her disappointment at losing her mother's support was lessened by Sarah's suggestion that she take Herbert back with her. When Gowan reappeared a little while later to announce that he had arranged for Reginald to take his mother-in-law to the station, the fact that he had presumed Sarah was going confirmed that he had not forgotten the previous evening's discussion.

When he was asked if he had any objection to Herbert going with her he simply retorted, 'Whitby folks' meddling's done t' lad no good, but I doubt a little more of it'll mek much difference. His absence'll help his mother.'

Sarah and a delighted Herbert left.

The day after their departure was a memorable one for reasons that had nothing to do with the Pickerings or the Booths. A snowstorm covered the moors in a white mantel and Lily admitted she found it frightening. 'How do we cope, Fran?' she asked.

'We have stores of all the basic foodstuffs, and we've managed in the past, Lily. Gowan has never let us down.'

'But you could give birth at any time,' a sceptical Lily retorted. 'What if you need Dr Ross?'

'Gowan says I'll be alright, Lily. After all, this is my fourth pregnancy. Don't worry. We'll manage ... we always do.'

A couple of days later, Fran announced, 'I have a feeling we're going to find out how well we'll cope with a new arrival and inclement weather, Lily.'

'You think your baby's on its way?' Lily looked terrified. 'How can you tell?'

'Well, my backache isn't necessarily labour pains and could be something else, but I doubt it. I think it's the baby.'

'In that case, I'll take over.' But Lily soon discovered that 'taking over' was not that easy. Chickens she could cope with, collecting eggs was enjoyable, but milking was quite different. She was completely out of her depth. To Kathleen's amusement, she sat awkwardly on a milking stool and tentatively reached for the cows udders. No matter how hard she tried to emulate what she had seen others do, the cow would not give its milk.

'You're not firm enough with it, Auntie,' Kathleen advised. 'Or perhaps the cow doesn't know you.'

'That's ridiculous!' Lily retorted. 'How can a cow refuse to give its milk because it's not familiar with someone?'

'It can,' replied a chuckling Kathleen. 'Father says cows are very sensitive creatures, and must be treated with respect if they are to give the best milk.'

As Lily seethed inwardly at Gowan's greater understanding of his cows than of his wife, Fran joined them. In spite of her discomfort, she looked somewhat pityingly at Lily and simply said, 'Don't worry, Lily. I'll take over.'

To Lily's shame, Fran reached over her distended and awkward abdomen and milked the cow. The effect was almost immediate: it brought on her first labour pains.

Lily took the milk to the dairy while her sister retired to the house. When Gowan was told of the impending birth, he announced that he had made arrangements with his brother William's wife, Mary, to help. He would send one of the labourers to Low Flask Farm with a message, but when there was news of the birth of his son, he and William would be at the Flask Inn.

The effect of Gowan's words on an already tense Lily were cataclysmic. She shook and her face reddened. She held her tiny frame erect, threw her head back and faced him squarely.

'Have you no thought for anyone but yourself?' she raged. 'Do you never consider the possibility that Fran might have an opinion – that she might have a preference for who helps her at a time like this? Do you always make decisions regardless of other's feelings? You view your wife as little more than your handmaiden. Are you not more concerned when your horse is in foal, or your cow in calf, than when your wife is about to give birth to your child? Even your daughter, Kathleen speaks of your care for your cows. I never hear her speak of your care for her mother.'

Lily drew a deep breath and her tone became sarcastic. 'If Fran should have need of a doctor's help, you will be found at the inn! And you know your baby will be a boy, do you? I know that girls warrant little attention in your world, but they are the ones who grow up to cook your food, care for your home, bear your children, tend your needs.

'I never had much sympathy with my sister Rose's suffragette inclinations, but I am beginning to accept her view that women are simply second-class citizens in the eyes of bigots and bullies like you. I implore you to take more care of the kind, sensitive woman you call your wife. Thorney Brow might be your inher-

162

itance, but it is her cross to bear. She works harder than the fishermen's wives in Whitby, harder than a charwoman, and has few comforts and little assistance. As we speak, she is racked with labour pain. Are you not concerned for her welfare?'

For a moment, Gowan hesitated. He towered above Lily's diminutive figure, his athletic form contrasting with her delicate frame, his roughened hands with her slender fingers, and his weather-beaten features with her clear, pale skin. The difference in their ages was obvious, nearly twenty-five years, but the difference in their backgrounds was a chasm.

Suddenly, his characteristic laugh boomed through the air and he cheerfully announced, 'Yon lass'll be fine wi' t' help of Mary, and it's about time I had a decent son – one who'll be of use to me on t' farm. Don't worry, Lily! You, little woman, will be at your best playing wi' t' girls. You might even manage to turn Kathleen into a proper pretty female. But I'll thank you to consider your own inadequacies before you look at mine. You've not had children. You're not even married. You're spoilt by your doting parents and I think a good dose of reality would make you a judge more worthy of my attention.

'Stop being so melodramatic, woman! You have no idea what you're talking about. Fran's simply doing what women do when they marry healthy, virile men. We all know that childbirth presents risks, but so do a lot of the things I have to do on t' farm. She'll be fine.'

Still chuckling, he turned. As he left, he said, 'I wish you a good evening, ladies. Make sure I'm told when my new son arrives!'

Lily burst into tears. 'How do you put up with that man?' she sobbed, but instead of a consoling phrase from Fran, she heard a deep groan. She saw her sister gasp as her waters broke on the flagstone floor of the kitchen. The baby was on its way.

The effect was dramatic. An event that Lily had never witnessed before was happening, and her resolve wavered as she began to think that Gowan was probably right. She was out of her depth, and had no idea how to help. How she wished her mother was there. How she wished she had gone back to Whitby. How she wished she had indulged in a little more gossip with the girls of the town who seemed so much more worldly-wise than her.

Her hands shook and she perspired as she sat with Fran at the kitchen table and asked what she could do to help.

Some time later, there was a loud knock on the door as Mary Pickering arrived. Her solidly built figure, wrapped in a heavy woollen shawl, gave an immediate impression of competence, and her broad smile and familiarity with her surroundings calmed Lily's panic-stricken nerves. She came in without further invitation and placed a basket containing a fruit cake, a bottle of whisky and an assortment of what looked like farming equipment on the table.

She looked at the scene before her and cheerfully announced, 'I think I timed that rather well, Fran!' To Lily, she said, 'Put t' kettle on, lass. I think we all need a nice cup of tea. I certainly do – t' weather's terrible. It's a good job William and Gowan have cleared t' tracks or we'd ha' never got through.'

The light faded and the animals in the farm accommodation shuffled, complained and eventually settled. A promising pink sky darkened, and the squabbling chatter of birds in the hedgerows and trees was replaced with the gentle rustle of mice, rats and voles in the undergrowth and the occasional hoot of an owl. Shadows in the windows of the inn silhouetted men relaxing.

Fran's labour intensified. Pains in her back and abdomen came in spasms and she felt shaky, but she was glad of Mary's presence. Mary's confident, homely figure was in stark contrast to Lily's look of sheer terror.

At last, as the clock struck midnight, she gave a penetrating scream of agony, gripped Mary's hand so tightly that even she winced and threw all pretence of dignity aside. Lying on the bed, her legs wide apart and drawn up to her body, she began to push her baby into the world.

'Look,' Mary told Lily, 'there's t' bairn's head.'

Lily gazed in wonder.

'Come on, lass! You can do it.' Mary's encouragement seemed to mean nothing to Fran, who was lost in her own distress, but her natural urge to push soon produced more of the baby's head. One last howl of pain led to a sudden change. It happened so quickly that Lily later swore that if she had blinked, she would have missed it.

A tiny baby girl was born, her whole body covered in white mucus streaked with blood. Mary deftly caught the little body, disentangled the cord and wiped the infant clean. Tears fell from both Fran and Lily's eyes as the baby gave its first cry.

'I don't believe in interfering wi' nature unless I have to,' Mary announced. 'We'll wait a while for t' afterbirth and, wi' a bit o' luck, we'll not have to cut t' cord too soon. I'm a believer in the need for t' mother's goodness to keep feeding t' baby until nature says its work is done.'

Turning her attention to Fran, she said, 'Tha's a bit torn, lass. It's amazing how a little scrap like that baby can tear a woman's skin. Tha'll have to expect a bit o' discomfort for a while.'

To Lily she said, 'As for you, lass. Go and get t' whisky bottle and a nice slice of cake. I can't decide which of you two is most in need of it, but it'll not hurt any of us to toast the baby's health.'

Fran was exhausted, but she gazed at her new baby in wonder as Mary urged her to take a drink of whisky. She refused and closed her eyes, but there was to be no rest. Yet again she had an urge to push and, although the pain was not as intense as it had

165

been, she could not relax until, finally, the afterbirth came away.

Armed with a pair of clippers used for cutting bacon and a pail from one of the outhouses, Mary tied a piece of twine around the cord near the baby's navel, cut the cord neatly away, put the mess of afterbirth in the pail and gently positioned towelling strips to absorb Fran's bleeding.

She wrapped the baby in a blanket and, having made sure mother and baby were comfortable, gave Lily a knowing look. 'I think you and I would be better to let that poor lass have a bit of rest.'

They retired to the kitchen. Lily felt as if she were in a dream. Nothing before had had this effect on her. The wonder of new birth with its agony, its ugliness and its beauty left her drained of emotion, exhausted by the newness of the experience.

Unlike her sister, she accepted Mary's offer of whisky and sat in silence. She was unsure whether she would ever want to go through such a trial herself, and wondered at the bravery of those women who had never tried to impress with their own experiences, and simply seemed to view them as part of the married state.

'Mary,' she murmured, 'how have you managed to go through this on twelve occasions? How does the body cope with such pain, such torture? I don't believe Fran is as strong as you. I'm in awe of the wonder of new life, but it takes such a toll on women. I'm not sure I ever want to marry now that I have seen this. I think I am going to remain a spinster!'

Mary chuckled. 'Nonsense, lass! Tha'll change tha' mind. And don't ask for miracles. 'Tis a woman's lot to bear children. All you can do is pray that there are not too many difficulties and thank the Good Lord that Fran's baby looks healthy enough. They'll both be fine.'

Meanwhile Gowan and William were at the Flask Inn, where they were well known. Their hosts, the Russell family who ran the establishment, also farmed the land around it. Not only did they offer hospitality with some good ales, whisky and gin, but could also talk knowledgeably about the land, weather, crops, livestock and prices at market.

Theirs was a popular venue. Unlike the taverns, public houses and inns of the town, their remote location meant that they were seldom subjected to scrutiny by the local authorities. Consequently they had their own rules for opening hours, weights and measures and appropriate ages for drinking. Mrs Russell was the licensee; if early starts on the farm meant that the men of the household needed to retire to bed, she could be relied on to continue serving until the customers chose to leave.

On the night when Fran was giving birth, the brothers took advantage of the Flask's lax opening hours and sat with their ale in a comfortable corner discussing their farms, the weather and the progress, or lack of it, of the war.

As the evening wore on other patrons left to make their way back to their farms but William was determined to keep his brother company, regardless of the demands on his time the following morning. By midnight, they were the only ones left.

They agreed that, considering the war was of no interest to anyone they knew, it was having a pretty devastating effect on manpower, but they also agreed that it had done them well for profit.

'I canna' understand why anyone would want to fight,' commented William, 'and especially if it involved the sea. T' waves are enough to deal with wi'out an enemy! T'other side's in no better position. Their lads don't want to fight either, and I hear they're manning German submarines by sending sailors aboard at the point of a gun. At least they're not doing that to our lads. Our lads'll fight and mek us proud.'

'Aye! Tha's right,' Gowan agreed. 'But don't run off wi' t' idea that they're doing it for king and country, or for the generals and captains in charge. They went for adventure, but they're fighting for their pals, for t'other lads who are in t' same boat and who they want to protect.'

The brothers drank another draught of ale and Gowan remarked, 'Have you heard about the women queueing up to work in arms factories? There's talk of townies turning up in cars wi' fur coats and luxury shoes shouting, "We want to make bullets to kill Germans!"'

'I hope they don't let them, brother,' William replied. 'If there were less bullets, there'd be no war. But do you realise a lot of them are the same silly women who weep over a picture of a pretty child or a dead bird!'

'Women!' Gowan gave a look of deep understanding. 'They've got no ability to reason. No reasoning at all! We tend our cattle, horses, pigs and sheep, we help them to bring new life into t' world, yet we're told to keep out o' t' way when our own wives give birth. I've never seen a woman birthing but I know one thing – it canna' be that different from t'other beasts God made.'

'My wife'll send word as soon as she returns home to Low Flask Farm,' William reassured his brother. 'Tha'll be wanting a boy, I expect.'

'Naturally,' Gowan answered without hesitation. 'I doubt there are many men who want to be surrounded by females! My wife might have grown up wi sisters and in t' town, but she's a fine lass. She's keen to learn the ways of the countryside and a good worker, good mother and an obedient wife.

'Do you know, William, that mother of hers wanted me to stay in the house tonight? Has she no idea? What man would stay in the house when his wife's in labour? What man would suffer the indignity of "keeping out of the way" under his own roof? And they keep insisting that Fran might need a doctor! You've never had the terrible misfortune of losing a wife in childbirth, William, but I can tell you honestly that a doctor was called for when my Tamar died and he could do nothing. I trust your Mary a lot more than any medical man who charges a fortune and does no good, so I'd not be going to Robin Hood's Bay to fetch Dr Ross!

'My other infant children are to be cared for by Lily. What part do I have to play? Truthfully, I am at a loss to know how to handle those Whitby women at times. They always seem to take on board the latest fads about doctors, women with opinions, and the rights of everyone except their husbands. I'm an old-school man. I want everyone to know their place, and my place is as head of the family. I take the responsibility that goes with that role, and I'll not have the likes of them questioning me. You're lucky, William, you've got farming blood on both sides of your family. You'll get a sight more respect than ever I do!'

William was about to agree with his brother and suggest that it might ease his suffering if they ordered another drink when Walter arrived.

The little boy who had been in Fran's schoolroom and had struggled over his books had grown to be a healthy, strong fourteen year old, an asset to the farm. Now he had been entrusted to ride to the Flask with important news. It was dark because the waxing moon was not yet full, and a bank of cloud allowed only a soft grey light to illuminate his difficult journey through the snow, but the boy was a competent rider.

He arrived, burst into the bar and announced that, 'Uncle Gowan's t' father of a baby girl.' Mrs Russell promptly offered Gowan a glass of gin, William a whisky, and Walter, ale. They drank a toast, William cheerfully clinking Gowan's glass as he congratulated him.

The party broke up. Gowan kicked his horse to a trot as he rode back to Thorney Brow, where he went straight to the bed-

169

room to inspect his new daughter. Fran shyly presented her baby to its father. Gowan agreed she was a pretty little thing and laughed at his own error in assuming she would be a boy. 'I've no ideas for naming a girl,' he said. 'Perhaps I better leave this one for you, Fran.'

Fran's response was immediate. 'I'd like to call her Lilian,' she said. 'Oh, Gowan, poor Lily was so unnerved by her experience today that I felt sorry for her. She meant so well. Please don't be offended by her outburst to you – she was quite out of her depth. But I would like to show her my love by giving this baby a name like hers. I think she would be well pleased with the compliment.'

Gowan smiled. 'I'll not stand in tha' way, lass. And this little mite could well be a dainty little creature that more resembles her Aunt Lily than either of the others.'

When Lily retired that night, she felt a warm glow of satisfaction. The baby had been named after her; Fran had withstood the ordeal of childbirth; Gowan appeared to have forgotten her outburst, and she could return to Whitby as soon as the weather permitted in the knowledge that she had been part of an event about which she had previously been woefully ignorant. She decided that, in future, she would take more notice of Rose and the rather eccentric women with whom she seemed to mix.

SIXTEEN

THE EARLY PART of 1915 witnessed a confused populace in Britain coming to terms with the fact that the 'brave boys' of the armed forces had not come home by Christmas. Stories of tragedies at sea and of a gruelling stalemate on the Western Front eradicated the wild enthusiasm of the early months of the war.

Newspaper photographs of trenches, submarines, Zeppelins and sunken vessels replaced images of troops waving flags as they rode into battle, of Britannia ruling the waves, and of humble opposition fighters laying down their arms at the prospect of facing Britain's finest. Casualties were being counted in numbers never before considered, and methods of waging war were changing beyond recognition. Men who had fought in, or who remembered, the Boer War talked of using aircraft being classed as a war crime, and declared that using poison gas was 'dirty tactics'. This was a totally new type of warfare and it would affect every household in the land.

In the female-dominated Booth household, Sarah and Rose were supportive of the wartime coalition. With their unshakable devotion to Asquith and Lloyd George, they were fiercely in favour of sending as many men to fight as the nation could offer.

'Just look how fit the boys are when they come home on leave!' Rose remarked. 'The war might not have ended as quickly as we hoped, but many lads look much better for their time in the army. It's because they get fed. I think I'll spend some time going round as many of the meeting places in Whitby that I can – pubs, markets, anywhere – encouraging more of them to join up.'

'I notice that your husband has not yet offered his services!' Lily's tone was sarcastic and her face implied disgust at her sister's declaration.

'My George would have been one of the first to enlist if it weren't for his troublesome back,' Rose countered.

Lily looked sceptical.

'I'm sure George would have done his best, dear,' intervened a tired-looking Sarah, and the subject was closed.

But Lily had a deeper reason for annoyance at George's apparent reluctance to risk his life. Her young man, Bert, was now a lieutenant in the Navy. She had seen him before he left for his last mission and she feared for his life.

At the Mission to Seamen, she had enjoyed hosting troops who were billeted in the town whilst they trained in the surrounding countryside. They had a reputation for being a bit too eager to partner local girls at the town's dances and social functions, but they'd formed a choir and she loved working with them. It was from them and from seamen that she heard stories of tragedy and hardship. To Lily, the war was now personal and she dreaded it continuing. She refused to encourage enlistment, and she prayed not so much for success in the war but for its end.

'I see they're advertising for women workers all over the place these days,' John commented.

'Proof at last that women are capable of doing more than housework!' Rose was delighted. 'It's a pity we had to have a war to make the point!'

'We're simply breeding a nation of malcontents!' Sarah looked annoyed. 'A woman's place is in the home. But at least the war has shown that there's no need for young lads to stay at school when they've no liking for it. That new-fangled idea might have been well-intentioned but it was always questionable. They can leave early now, providing they help with the war effort.' She added hastily, 'Of course, that would never apply to our Herbert. He's such a bright little thing, a real candidate for the grammar school, if ever there was one.'

On Fylingdales, the war barely affected life during the early months of the year. The Staintondale Hunt had met in February, and a wild, invigorating ride on hard earth on a dry day was followed by a convivial evening. That same week, Gowan represented the farming community of Fylingdales at the Whitby Licensed Victuallers Annual Dinner. He often chuckled when he remembered it. A toast to the king had been drunk reverently, but a toast to the Whitby District magistrates was greeted with hilarity. Their laxity in enforcing legal opening hours meant that the inns on Fylingdales stayed open for as long as the licensees liked, regardless of wartime restrictions. Similarly, a toast to the Whitby District brewers and wine and spirits merchants was greeted with the stamping of feet, the clink of glasses and the banging of tables, for they were infamous for evading the regulations about premises and age limits for the sale of alcohol. The best toast, according to Gowan, had been the one to Lloyd George where they thanked him for not striking them down.

'Silly little Welshman!' Gowan exclaimed. 'T' man's got no inkling of family responsibility. T' state'll do this and t' state'll do that. Who does he think he is? Nanny to t' world? Here, we look after our own!'

The war become more personal when news arrived of the *Rohilla* disaster. 'Those brave lads from Ruswarp are going to get a reward, I hear,' William said to his brother as they worked in the fields.'

'And no more than they deserve, brother,' Gowan answered. 'To rescue the crew of the *Rohilla* was a truly heroic thing. But I tell you, William, I'd not be in their shoes, reward or no reward. To convert a ship into a hospital ship, send it out to sea and then put the lights out on the lighthouses so the poor sods didn't know where they were and ran aground in a gale... well! I ask you! It's another piece of lunacy from our so-called betters.'

'At least we can do our bit and stay safe!' William chuckled.

'True,' Gowan smiled. 'And I can't see our lads faring badly, can you?'

'Well, three o' mine are in t' army now.' William looked proud. 'Gowan's in t' Veterinary Corp, Thomas is in t' Medical Corp, and young Christopher's thinkin' o' going to sea ... but I can't imagine that!'

'Tha' knows my Gowan's wi' t' army, too,' Gowan replied.

'T' eldest are growin' up fast, brother,' William remarked. 'Why it's only this year that my lad, Francis, was married, and you've got a wedding in your family coming up soon.'

Gowan nodded. 'I'll not be forgetting that!' he chuckled. 'My Reginald's been courting Eliza Beeforth for long enough now. She's a fine lass from a good moors' family. They'll do us all proud.'

The warmth of spring on the moors saw the release of animals onto pasture and the sowing of crops for the forthcoming season. From landowner to the humblest farm worker, all were witness to the promise of new life. Common seals came ashore to nurture their young, curlews gave their distinctive call and lapwings offered spectacular aerobatic displays high on the moors. In every household there was an expectation of better days to come.

At Thorney Brow, the new baby was proving a delicate child. Gowan's sister-in-law, Mary, had not only been there when the baby was born but she encouraged her daughter, Elizabeth, to help and the girl was a huge support during Fran's lying-in.

'There's many a babe looked as fragile as yon Lilian,' Mary had remarked shortly before the day of Reginald's wedding. 'Wait 'till t' time comes for her t' eat good, wholesome food and she'll thrive. You mark my words and stop tha' frettin',' she reassured. 'Just gi' t' little scrap some time.'

Fran had taken her sister-in-law's advice and started spoon feeding Lilian with bread soaked in milky tea. She wasn't convinced that there had been any noticeable improvement and, when the day came for Reginald's marriage, Gowan went alone.

The ceremony was at St Stephen's Church and the pews were filled with well-wishers. Reginald, now a sturdy twenty-four year old, had inherited some of his father's presence and stood proudly in front of the altar waiting for his bride. As her father, George, walked Eliza down the aisle, he gave Gowan a broad smile. Later, the two men sat comfortably at the Falcon Inn discussing their farms and, above all, the war.

'Tha's given those two a fine dresser for their nuptials, Gowan,' George remarked. 'That must have set you back a bob or two. I doubt our fathers could ha' given us the like of it when we were wed!'

'Tha's not been ungenerous tha' sen,' Gowan responded, and the two men chuckled. Both were benefiting from the soaring prices that accompanied the wartime blockade that prevented foreign imports of food.

'I'm thinkin' o' makin' a little investment in property,' Gowan said. 'Has tha' thought on doin' t' same, George?'

'Nay, lad, I'll stick to what I'm comfortable wi'!' George was quick to respond. 'Tha's had t' example o' tha' mother, Gowan. She's bin a formidable woman wi' t' finances. I guess that's why tha's at Thorney Brow. 'Tis a fine property, and hearsay has it tha' pays a very reasonable rent. I'm not so blessed. But I wish thee luck. What did tha' have in mind?'

'I'm buying number 2 The Esplanade in Robin Hood's Bay.'

The two men toasted each other's good luck and Gowan felt a tingle of excitement. He was about to be more than a respected farmer; He would be a man of property.

But a highlight in Gowan's life came when, without warning, a khaki-uniformed figure strolled down the path to Thorney Brow one afternoon in April. It was his son, Gowan, on leave from service with the Prince of Wales' Own Regiment.

Young Gowan arrived at shearing time. Shepherding was the one aspect of farming that Gowan and William Pickering viewed as a joint venture. At that time of year, they took their dogs on to the moors and drove their flock to Thorney Brow where there was more space than at Low Flask Farm where William lived. Here they clipped fleeces, removed maggots, marked ears and castrated young male lambs. Ewes were driven in to an enclosure for lambing, and animals not yet ready for mating or slaughter were sent back to the moors.

At the moment when young Gowan arrived, they were wielding heavy-duty scissors and ear punches. William remarked, 'T' tup's done us proud this year,' as he confirmed another ewe was pregnant.

'Aye, he's a fine fellow,' Gowan agreed. 'Yon flock'll be bigger next year, thanks to him. Prices for lamb and wool are both up again.' He wiped the sweat from his brow, released a heavy but well-clipped animal back to join the flock and was about to collect another when a familiar voice called, 'Wanting another hand, Father?'

Both Gowan and William stopped work. Broad grins spread across their faces. A sheep that William had just captured struggled back to her feet and, unclipped, re-joined the others. William's son, Henry, shouted from the yard where he was stacking fleeces onto a wagon ready for market, and Ernest peered out from the cowshed, saw his brother and abandoned a cow that was birthing.

A loud 'hurrah' went up. Fran, hearing the noise from the side of the house where she was taking advantage of the dry weather to hang out the washing, ran to see what was happening. Other than Ernest, who reluctantly returned to care for the cow he had been tending, all thoughts of the day's work were abandoned.

The family crowded into the kitchen where young Gowan, now twenty-one years old, stood proudly in his uniform. He was the centre of attention. Fran hugged him, his father shook his hand, tea was poured, and fruit cake and cheese offered.

The family stood in awe as he told them a little of his life. The familiar twinkle in his eyes was still there, and his sense of humour still brought laughter, but there was a new, more mature side to his nature. The boy who had left with such enthusiasm and joyous zeal was now a man, and one who had experienced more of life – and perhaps of death – than he would admit to.

Almost immediately, talk turned to the use of horses in the war. Gowan Junior described fine beasts being reduced to emaciated, ill-cared-for nags, men weeping as they saw their best mounts pulling huge loads in filthy, squalid conditions, and other horses left to die in agony. The ammunition needed to put them out of their misery was reserved for Germans.

When his son left to visit the Burnett family, Gowan was seething with anger. 'If all t' lads who went to war were like that son o' mine, t' war'd be over in no time – but it'd be no thanks to t' idiots who claim to know what they're doing on a battlefield. Most on 'em are trained at fancy schools, spend all their time wi' maps and diagrams, parade around in ridiculous uniforms wi' fancy braid, and then tell t' poor sods what to do when they don't know what they're doing themselves. T' yeomen of England are a fine breed, but we've got some idiots to lead us wi' no real love o' horses. And didn't t' lad say as some are likely to be sent to the Dardanelles? Instead of worrying about what t' Turks are up to, we'd be better concentrating on stopping an invasion of Britain.' He stormed back outside.

Gowan escorted his son to the Falcon Inn that evening

where they joined neighbours, friends and members of the hunt. Despite the distances between the farms, the news had spread quickly amongst the moorland folk, who thought fondly of young Gowan's prowess as a farm worker, his skill as a rider and huntsman, his good nature, and his association with both Howdale and Thorney Brow farms.

In the smoky and dimly lit tap room, they drank his health and that of the British armed forces, in particular the boys from Fylingdales. Gowan Junior was the first Pickering boy to serve with the armed forces who had been seen since they had enrolled. As he related his stories, the atmosphere in the room became increasingly fraught.

The farming community spoke as one in their condemnation of the treatment of horses. Henry Noble ventured that some of the officers should be shot, old Mr Martindale assured them that horses had been highly prized in previous conflicts, and John Russell swore he would never send another animal to help in the war effort.

They drank to the yeomen of England, and they drank to their sons' health and welfare. Late in the evening, they made their way home across darkened moorland where their horses needed no guidance and their families were already in bed.

◆ ◆ ◆

As spring days turned to summer, Gowan invested in new hogs; he considered lard a necessity, and these animals were bred for their fat. He bought seed potatoes, fertiliser, a good quality heifer, and he ordered a threshing machine.

Fran suggested the family would benefit from a paraffin cooker to supplement the huge range she used, which was stifling hot in summer. She was thrilled when Gowan not only bought the cooker but a whisk, the likes of which she had never seen before.

They agreed that 1915 was a good time in their lives. Were it not for the continued shortage of labour, which involved housing itinerant workers, and the problems associated with their lack of competence, life could scarcely have been better.

As spring turned to summer and warm rain promised good pasture for cattle, the occasional thunderstorm did little to dampen the spirits of the farming community. They could see the aurora at the beginning of August from the dark remoteness of the moors, and Gowan insisted that it was a good omen.

On a particularly fine day, two of the Staintondale Hunt members visited Thorney Brow to collect the dogs to form a pack. Gowan and Reginald decided to go with them. The summer hunts helped to rid the land of cubs and simultaneously trained young dogs for the later events that would concentrate on fully-grown foxes. Fran had learned that 'trencher-fed' dogs might be anathema to her family, but feeding and caring for them at home meant that the hunt avoided the costs of maintaining kennels.

As she watched her husband leave with his dogs, she knew that the camaraderie and the exhilaration of the ride would give him temporary release from the constant demands of the farm.

Herbert was absent; to his father's annoyance, he had pleaded to spend some of his school holiday at Flowergate, though he had promised to be back in time to help with the harvest. Kathleen had begged to join the hunt. As he affectionately ruffled her hair, Gowan promised that she would soon be old enough to mount the pony he had in mind for her and join in. Annie followed her big sister everywhere and, as soon as their father had gone, the two little girls went out to the fields to play.

Baby Lilian was still proving difficult; her constant sickness after food and her frail appearance were a worry. But with only the baby at home and the rest of the family happily occupied, the farmhouse was tranquil and pleasant. Fran collected produce from her garden, gazed across the rough pasture towards the coast, smelled the freshness of the sea, listened to gentle lowing of cattle and felt content.

The little scene of domesticity was disturbed as a figure clad in a postman's uniform trotted his horse down the incline from the moors and into the yard. Fran immediately ran to him, for letters were unusual. He handed her an envelope addressed to Gowan, doffed his cap politely and left. It was official looking, marked with the Ministry of Defence stamp. She could not open it for it was addressed to her husband, and she could not tell him of its arrival because he was somewhere across the moors. She doubted he would be home before evening.

'Oh, God! Please let it not be what I think it is,' she murmured and went into the house. The day had lost its splendour; the sky's blue faded. The sights, sounds and smells that had so entranced her only minutes earlier had gone. She placed the letter carefully on the kitchen table and sat, alone and unsure. Only the ticking clock disturbed the silence, its regular beat reminding her that time passes slowly when action is curtailed.

Fran was distracted when she did the evening milking, and she gave the children a perfunctory tea of bread, ham and milk. She gazed at her daughters. Sturdy Kathleen had inherited her father's athletic figure, energy and enthusiasm for life; Annie's stocky little body exuded a love of home and good food; Lilian was a delicate little creature but gave no indication that her tendency to sickness was life-threatening. Yet each was so fragile, so unaware of life's challenges and so precious. She prayed that they would be spared the tragedies that life so randomly inflicted, and that the frightening envelope on the kitchen table might contain nothing of any significance.

She prepared a meal for Gowan in a desultory manner, sent the children to bed and then waited. At last, horses' hooves clattered into the yard. Gowan's dogs ran ahead of him as he took his horse to its stable, released it from its harness and rubbed it down.

She joined him. His usual 'Now then, lass' sounded puzzled as he noticed her face. In silence, she led him in to the kitchen and handed him the letter. He tore it open. She had no need to ask if it was what she had expected. He sank into a chair, put his head in his hands and silently passed it to her.

The letter read,

Dear Mr Pickering,

I regret very much to inform you that your son, Private Gowan Pickering Number 17457 of the Prince of Wales' Own Regiment was posted as missing, presumed dead, on the ninth day of the month of August 1915.

The company was taking part in an assault as part of our campaign in the Balkan theatre and he was integral to our efforts in Gallipoli.

It was signed by a captain whose name meant nothing to either Gowan or Fran. They did not care; the content was sufficient for them to come to terms with, and the detail was meaningless. There was silence.

Gowan was the first to speak and his voice suddenly seemed charged with energy. 'What do they mean – missing, presumed dead?' he said. 'Don't they know what's going on in their own battlefield? They can't presume he's dead. Why, we saw young Gowan for ourselves! He was healthy, ready to fight. No, Fran. He'll turn up right as rain, tha'll see for tha' sen. This is a mistake and, mark my word, I'll get even with the idiot who made it.'

He began pacing the floor and started listing the people he would contact. He suggested getting on his horse immediately and seeking out the recruiting officer in Whitby, who could tell him the addresses he would need to file a letter of protest. He suggested catching a train to York the next day to visit a barracks where information might be available. He poured himself a glass of gin and read and re-read the letter.

Fran knew that there was no mistake. She felt out of her depth but decided the best course of action was to let his anger take its course. Gradually Gowan's outburst became less frantic, his voice less confident and suddenly his mood changed. With a deep, heart-rending sigh, he sat down heavily on a kitchen chair and said quietly, 'It's true isn't it, Fran? Gallipoli was a blood bath wasn't it?' She nodded her head. 'I'm goin' to hang on to t' thought that t' lad might be alive but 'tis an unlikely thing.'

Gowan's complexion was ashen and his hands shook. He was a man defeated and all his anger had gone, his fighting spirit dissipated. Fran put her arm around his shoulders as he talked. He wished he had persuaded his son to stay on the farm, fought to stop him leaving home. He wished that he had shown the boy more appreciation, that he was valued. He hoped that his brother's sons would be safe, that the killing would end and life could go back to the way it had been.

At last he gave in to the emotion that had driven him to anger and, for the first time in her life, Fran saw him weep. She knew they would cling to the possibility that there would be a miracle – that the boy would be found alive – but she also knew that this was unlikely. As the sun set and darkness descended across the moors, they joined as one in their sadness.

SEVENTEEN

SARAH BOOTH INSPECTED her home carefully. George, the grandfather clock, was ticking his steady way through time; the chairs in the parlour had clean, lace antimacassars across their backs, and the gateleg table was pushed against the wall but ready to serve its purpose and was covered with a broderie anglaise tablecloth. The mantelpiece displayed the busts of two Negroes her father had carved out of jet, a pretty china figurine and photographs of the family.

On this cold March evening a glowing fire warmed the room and created flickering images on the walls. Polished brass oil lamps emitted a gentle light that complemented the heavy red and gold velvet curtains that were Sarah's pride and joy. Unlike houses she had previously lived in, they covered high sash windows in the Georgian style that were very much to her taste.

Her daughter joined her. 'You know, Mary,' she commented, 'I think 50 Flowergate is looking rather fine. I know my sisters appreciate it, though I'm sure they'll find something to criticise!'

Mary gave a wry smile. 'You might well be right, but the war's been going on for two years now and our poor boys in uniform have been suffering the winter weather. That should give them something other than us to talk about.'

The doorbell rang. Mary answered, helped the visitors to relieve themselves of their outdoor clothing and ushered them into the front parlour.

'Thank you, Mary.' Sarah nodded her appreciation to her daughter then turned to her sisters, gave each a token kiss on the cheek and enquired after their health. As they waited for Mary to return with tea, they chatted about the weather and the seasonal proliferation of coughs and colds.

When Mary returned and the tea had been poured, the atmosphere changed. Polly sat very upright in her chair and remarked, 'So Hannah is to be married!' She exuded an air of disapproval.

'Yes,' Sarah replied. 'I was as taken aback as you! She's well past the age when a woman can bear children but, lo and behold, she has surprised us all.'

'And the lucky gentleman is a fisherman, is he not?'

'Yes.'

'Well, Emmie and I came here today especially to talk to you about this match. We know you too well. You're just not forthright enough, and we feel it our duty to do all that we can to ensure Hannah's welfare. Does the young man realise that he is marrying above his station? Please don't upset yourself if I speak my mind, but you surely have not forgotten that we are Pearsons – a family with a heritage to be proud of.'

'I have not forgotten, dear.' Sarah looked annoyed. She clasped her hands firmly together on her lap and threw back her head.

Emmie intervened. 'We are simply concerned for your family's welfare, Sarah. Hannah has always been such a good daughter and a huge asset to you. It would be a tragedy to see one so innocent being taken advantage of by any man. And we have very little knowledge of Mr Locker.'

Sarah rose to her daughter's defence. 'Thank you, dear sisters. I understand your concern but I have got to know Mr Locker and can vouch for his character. I'm quite sure he won't take advantage of Hannah, and I think we should rejoice that she's found a life companion and wish her good luck.'

Mary gave her mother a shy smile of gratitude and tried to

move the conversation away from her sister by offering her aunts a slice of parkin. Emmie looked delighted, remarking that parkin was always a treat. Polly, however, changed the subject when her eyes caught a glimpse of an addition to Sarah's collection of photographs. 'Tell me, Sarah, is that a photograph of dear Fran's children I see on your mantelshelf?'

Sarah beamed. She reached for the newly framed photograph and handed it to her sister. 'You noticed!' she said. 'Well, you know that Herbert and Kathleen stay with us here at Flowergate during term time. Lily brought Annie into town just before Christmas and I thought that I would have their likenesses taken whilst they were together. Isn't it lovely?' Her manner changed from being the apprehensive defender of her daughter's choice of husband to that of proud grandparent.

Both Emmie and Polly were immediately absorbed.

'They look really beautiful, Sarah ... so well dressed.'

'And so well fed. Just look at little Annie!'

'And I do believe Herbert's wearing that jumper you knitted.'

'Kathleen's a fine figure of a girl, isn't she?'

'Oh, Sarah, you must be so proud of them. But I really think it should be Gowan's job to have a photographer take pictures of his children. Am I right in thinking that you paid for this? Really, that man is dreadful! Not only does he take advantage of your kindness in taking in his children, but he even allows you to pay for their photograph. You're far too good to him, Sarah.'

Polly continued. 'He's got to be the most selfish, boorish man I've ever known. You poor dear, my heart goes out to you. And he's not your only problem. Hannah wants to marry a lowly fisherman, and Rose lives next door to you with a ne'er-do-well of a husband.'

Sarah looked annoyed but was quick to reply. 'Rose has always had a mind of her own, as you both know full well. Although it would be nice to see her with a man who can provide for her needs, at least I know that George is a gentle soul. He would never hurt her. But Fran is different and Gowan is different. Right now, I think we should refrain from any criticism of that man – he deserves nothing but sympathy. To live with the knowledge that your son might be dead but keep hoping that he could be alive is almost unimaginable.'

Polly and Emmie were silent. Mary gazed at her mother and was the first to speak. 'Lily went to see them. She says Gowan is not himself and he seemed to have aged. Poor Gowan – and poor Fran. Oh, this war's got a lot to answer for!'

Polly seemed determined to bring the subject back to an analysis of Sarah's family. 'Rose seems to think it's a war worth waging. Was she not mentioned in the Gazette as one of the sponsors of the Tobacco Fund? And I think you told us that she was trying to reproduce a copy of Kitchener's "Your Country Needs You" poster to put in her window.'

Mary giggled. 'You need have no fear that Rose would create a poster good enough to put in her window, Aunt Polly. Her artistic talents aren't up to that. Her so called "poster" went on the fire! And, yes, she has been collecting for the Tobacco Fund but I'm afraid that was a bit of a disaster as well, wasn't it, Mother?'

'Oh, really, dear. I'm sure your aunts don't want to hear about that!' Sarah tried to silence her.

'She surely didn't destroy the fund?' Emmie looked intrigued.

'No, no ... the fund did very well and that's why she got a mention in the paper,' Mary was keen to explain. 'The trouble was, she sold Father's scraps of fabric that he had saved for repairs and sent the money to the *Gazette*. Father always tells his clients to feel free to return to him with any problems if he's done tailoring work for them, but he only discovered when it was too late that he couldn't help them because the remnants had gone. He was very upset and Rose refused to apologise. She said the boys at the front deserved a bit of a treat, and the least we could do was send them tobacco.'

'There you are!' Polly looked triumphant. 'I told you Rose was a keen supporter of the war. That girl might have caused this family some headaches, but at least she's a true patriot. You, Sarah, seem less concerned about our boys in the trenches than about Gowan Pickering's son. He's not the only one, you know. There are families all across the land grieving for their losses. But we must stay resolute and win this war. As for Gowan Pickering, I hope you're not starting to sound like poor Fran who always seems to see his point of view. I really thought she had more about her. When she worked with me at my little school, she was such a capable girl. I just don't know what's happened to her. He's a dreadful man.'

Sarah's brow furrowed as she considered Polly's remark. 'I admit I'm beginning to re-assess him,' she said. 'He may represent much of what we find abhorrent – his liking for the hunt, his attachment to the Church of England, his predilection for alcohol – but his demeanour has changed since the news of his son arrived. I wonder if I've misjudged him. He has got feelings and he cares about his family. It was for Fran's benefit that he allowed the two eldest to come here to Whitby, for her health has been very indifferent. He didn't want them to come. And he pays their way, so I can't complain.'

Sarah smiled. ' I love having them here, you know. Although Kathleen freely admits she wishes she was back on the farm, she's very good at school when she puts her mind to it. And Herbert ... well he's doing so very well and loves school. It's a real privilege to be given such beautiful children to care for.'

Polly and Emmie gazed at Sarah in disbelief. 'You hated that man, Sarah,' Polly burst forth. 'I've seen you weep tears over poor Fran's fate and, for that matter, for the way he's treated you.'

Sarah busied herself with the teacups. 'I'll be honest,' she said. 'It could be that we've been too quick to judge. Fran always had a romantic, impractical streak, but perhaps my dreamy daughter actually made a good match. Gowan is so well thought of on the moors and he's becoming a wealthy man, even investing in property, I hear.'

'Fran is such a gentle soul and she deserves a good life. I do hope you're right, Mother,' Mary murmured, but her look of disbelief belied her words.

Polly and Emmie were less prepared to compromise their views.

'Mary's right,' Emmie said. 'But you'll never convince me that having baby after baby out on the moors, isolated, lacking support from family and friends, and dealing with inclement weather, recalcitrant animals and a husband who has more understanding of his horse than his wife is a satisfactory life for anyone.'

'One thing is for certain, it's in God's hands,' Sarah concluded. 'Perhaps it does us good sometimes to air our opinions but we all know that when a woman marries, she no longer has rights of her own. Poor Fran can only do one thing, try to be a good wife. And we can only hope that, despite our reservations, Gowan is a good husband.'

'I'm glad Rose isn't here,' Mary remarked. 'She has some very forceful views on the rights – or lack of them – of married women. It's a good job her George is too lazy to argue with her!'

Sarah heaved a sigh of relief. Mary's remark brought a lighter note to the discussion and Polly and Emmie chuckled at the idea of George's laziness in allowing his wife to voice controversial ideas. The atmosphere relaxed, the conversation moved to the time and place of Hannah's wedding, of Lily's part in it as organist at the church, and Lily's own choice of man.

Sarah opened a drawer in her bureau and rummaged amongst the papers she kept there. Beaming with pleasure, she handed two cuttings from the local paper to her sisters. They were dated

February and March 1916. Emmie immediately drew back and remarked that Polly would have to read them as she had brought her pince-nez.

Polly dutifully raised her head to get a good view and read: '*Herbert, eldest son of Mr. J Watson, Norton, passed the Board of Trade examination for Master Mariner at Sunderland.*'

And, in a second cutting: '*Herbert Watson has been granted a Master's Certificate at the Marine School of South Shields.*'

'You must be so proud of Lily, dear.' Polly smiled. 'Fancy her having a man like Herbert wanting to marry her. We met him once, if you remember, Sarah. He was good looking, pleasant and well mannered, the perfect suitor! We remarked at the time that Lily'd done well for herself. He didn't even seem to be daunted by their height difference. To be honest, we had to laugh for he's a good six foot and Lily can't even manage five!'

Both Polly and Emmie chuckled but Sarah squirmed. 'Can you never find anything to say about my daughters without making sure you include something derogatory?' she bristled. 'If it isn't Fran's way of life, it's Rose's husband or Hannah's fiancée – and now it's Lily's height! Are you two never happy unless you're finding fault? I really do despair of you.'

She turned to Mary. 'At least they've missed you out, dear!' she said. 'Perhaps it's because you're so good to us all. And perhaps it's time we had a fresh pot of tea.'

Mary dutifully rose to replenish the tea whilst Polly and Emmie retaliated.

'Nonsense, dear Sarah. You know we're only concerned for everyone's welfare.'

'Ridiculous! We only want what's best.'

'Oh dear, don't start getting over-sensitive. We've always prided ourselves on being truthful with each other. For heaven's sake, if we can't speak our minds when we're together, then when can we? Polite discourse is for polite society, not family.'

'You know we're always here for you, Sarah.'

As the ladies drank their tea they continued chatting but, to Sarah's relief, their remarks were no longer so personal. Emmie remarked that she'd read an account in the *Daily Mirror* about women leaping to their deaths off a steamer to avoid mines in the sea. Sarah put on a rather superior air and announced that she didn't read the *Daily Mirror*, she preferred *The Times*. Polly retaliated by saying, 'You're such a snob, dear,' and insisted that the *Mirror* had described very clearly the damage German Zeppelins had done to many of the buildings in Paris. She also remarked that she never understood why people wanted to go to Paris because the language was quite unintelligible.

'I'd rather go to Paris than Dublin,' Emmie said. 'The people of Ireland seem intent on civil war.'

'Thank goodness we live in Whitby,' Sarah concluded. 'The rest of the world seems very frightening at present. And whether you read *The Times* or the *Mirror*, it doesn't make the suffering incurred by this war any less painful.'

On that note, Polly and Emmie decided it was time they left. Mary collected their coats, hats and gloves. As they prepared for their journey home, Polly commented that surely British boys must be the best in the world.

'It was so sad when they had to be forced to volunteer, wasn't it?' Emmie remarked.

'Well, at least there's no argument now!' Polly reminded her. 'The Military Service Act means they'll have to join up whether they like it or not. I'm sure Mr Asquith will soon get all this trouble sorted out. He's a fine, steady, honest Yorkshireman, and the evacuation of Gallipoli is a step in the right direction. Progress is definitely being made. Anyway, we can't just lay down our arms and let the Hun do what they want!'

At last, Polly and Emmie left. Sarah gave Mary a knowing look. 'I love my sisters but they can be exhausting!' she remarked.

Mary smiled as they went into the kitchen to prepare the evening meal. 'Do you really think Mr Asquith is doing a good job, Mother? The war is dragging on so, and it's making such a difference to so many people's lives – and I don't mean a good difference, either!'

Sarah paused as she reached for a potato. 'I honestly don't know what to think, Mary. Rose came here a couple of days ago really upset. The young men she watched getting fit and healthy from their days in the forces seem to have changed. She'd seen a man whose leg had been partially amputated. Apparently, he'd suffered from 'trench foot' caused by constant exposure to cold, damp conditions in the trenches. The foot had become gangrenous. He won't work again and the likelihood is that he will face destitution. She says she's seen too many other families whose young men have returned very so different to when they left. They seem to undergo a transformation, and they become moody and sullen, or reclusive, or argumentative, and often they turn to drink. The war seems to have had a very strange effect on them. And then, of course, in our own family, we have poor Gowan.'

'You really feel sorry for him, don't you, Mother.' Mary looked concerned.

'Of course I do, dear. And I meant it when I said I wondered if we'd misjudged him. Oh, my! I really find I am so unsure about everything these days ... Fran and Gowan, Rose, the war.'

'Why Rose, Mother?' Mary looked quizzical.

'Oh, no ... not Rose herself but the things she's been saying. She's been making me think. She's been saying for years that women are capable of doing more than simply caring for their homes, and now, look at the work they are doing ... and doing well. Only the other day, someone remarked what a delight it was to have a woman delivery person. The lad who used to do deliveries for the butcher tended to throw the meat into your arms or sling it onto your kitchen table if the door was open. Now, a pleasant young lady carefully passes it to her customer and asks if everything is alright. And, I've noticed the postman is a woman and she handles the mail with real care.'

'But I think Rose also insisted that women should get paid at the same rate as the men used to be paid and they're not, are they, Mother?'

'Sadly, no!' Sarah responded, but then she looked pensive. 'Oh dear, Mary. I didn't tell my sisters but I am riddled with doubt. I'm even beginning to doubt dear Mr Asquith. Surely this war should have progressed further than it has. Polly and Emmie are not alone in viewing the evacuation of Gallipoli as a success, but Gowan and Fran won't see it like that, and my neighbours whose sons are away fighting don't see it like that! My biggest consolation is that I don't have a son to worry about.'

EIGHTEEN

EASTER 1916 SAW British troops on the Western Front deal with snow, sleet and driving rain. On Fylingdales the picture was very similar as remote farms and hamlets strove to deal with nature's worst.

Howdale School maintained its reputation for having the worst attendance record within the local authority's jurisdiction as the weather prevented pupils from crossing the moor. Fran took huge consolation from the fact that both Herbert and Kathleen were doing well at Cliff Street School in Whitby. She was pregnant again, and admitted that she was glad when, despite Kathleen's protests, they stayed in Whitby for the Easter holiday.

As soon as the worst storms were over, Sarah decided to visit Thorney Brow and see for herself how her daughter was faring. The station at Fyling Hall was closed due to the war, but the train driver was very accommodating. When the locomotive was forced to slow to walking pace as it negotiated the steep incline near Alison Head Wood, she jumped from the train, gave the guard a cheerful wave and walked the rest of the way. She enjoyed the fresh air, the sweet smell of the sea and the sight of acres of open heather moorland.

'A truly magnificent sight,' she thought. 'If only it was less demanding on the lives of those who call it home!'

The scene that greeted her as she walked into the kitchen of Thorney Brow farmhouse confirmed her thoughts. Unusually, the whole place appeared unkempt. Unwashed dishes and cooking pots cluttered the earthenware sink, and muddy footprints scarred the floor. The table had not been cleared from breakfast, and the smell of unwashed clothes, cooking and various animal and human effluent combined to create an unsavoury air.

Annie ran to greet her grandmother and the little girl mirrored the room. Her hair needed brushing, her hands and face needed washing, and her clothes appeared to have been on her little body for longer than was hygienic. Lilian was sleeping in the corner of the room, blissfully unaware of her chaotic surroundings.

Sarah stood rooted to the spot as she gazed around her and looked at her daughter who was standing next to the big kitchen table. Then she pulled herself together, greeted Annie with a hug and, looking into Fran's eyes, murmured, 'You poor, poor girl. Dear Fran, what is happening?'

Fran burst into tears. 'Oh, Mother, I feel so ill. Although my baby isn't due yet, I feel its weight and every movement it makes, and it drains my strength. It takes all the goodness from my body. It leaves me feeling wretched, so tired I can barely move and am incapable of doing anything about it. Just look at my home. Look at my children. Look at me!' Her body shook as she spoke between sobs.

Sarah rose to the challenge, threw back her shoulders, put down her portmanteau and announced, 'Well, it's a good job I'm here, isn't it!' Turning to Annie, she said, 'I think your mother needs a cup of tea. Why don't you go and find a nice cup and saucer and I'll put the kettle on?' Annie beamed and ran to do her grandmother's bidding.

By the time Gowan came into the house at the end of the day, Sarah had sent Fran to bed, tidied the kitchen, washed Annie and Lilian and made a meal. He looked exhausted. 'Now then, lass,' he said as he removed his dirty boots and sat at the kitchen table. 'Where's Fran?'

194

'I've sent her to bed, Gowan.' Sarah's face was drawn and anxious. 'She was in a dreadful state when I arrived. I've not seen her look so frail at this stage and I'm really worried about her. Has she been like this for long?'

Gowan looked annoyed. 'I suppose you're going to blame me for this, aren't you? You do realise, ma'am, that I've got a farm to run. I can hardly be expected to look after the household as well. And Fran's only got the two little ones to care for. What on earth more can I do? I pay good wages for help on the farm, but I don't think my labourers should be looking after the house and children as well! Why, it feels as if I'm supposed to work miracles these days!'

'No! I was not blaming you, Gowan, and the idea that I'm suggesting you work miracles is ridiculous – but something round here needs to change.' Sarah drew herself up to her full height and gave Gowan one of her superior looks. 'Perhaps you should pay for help for Fran, not just on the farm. What do you think?'

'No! I'm not doing that. We've always looked after our own here on the moors. I'm not bringin' in a stranger. It's not necessary. There's got to be a better way.'

'Well I'd like to know what it is!' Sarah's tone was scathing. 'And I hope that whatever you decide to do, you bear in mind that Herbert and Kathleen are supposed to be coming back here more regularly now that the weather's improved. Fran'll never cope with them as well as Annie and Lilian.'

'Well you might ha' noticed that young Lilian's eating a bit better. I had to tie that child to a chair and force-feed her perfectly good food to make her see t' error of her ways but I think I've succeeded. Now she puts morsels o' food in her mouth and keeps a wary eye on me at dinner! I do my bit, Sarah. I can do no more than mek t' little uns respect their parents.'

'Gowan – you miss my point. Lilian may be of concern, but

she's thriving, More importantly, Fran's not coping with the day-to-day running of the home. She's ill. She needs help.'

Gowan looked puzzled. 'Young Tamar might pop in,' he volunteered. 'T' Tyreman's ha' done a great job wi' t' lass, and now young Ethel's got her own way and she's joined them at Thorpe. Perhaps they could even tek it in turns to come to Thorney Brow.'

'Well Tamar must be fourteen or so by now, and Ethel's older, so they might be some use to Fran. Would you be able to fetch them, Gowan?'

'I'm not sure I could do that. Perhaps occasionally, but not on a regular basis. Nay! I canna' commit to that.'

The man looked exhausted. He looked older than the last time Sarah had seen him, which was only a matter of weeks before at Hannah's wedding. 'Let's have dinner and decide what's for the best,' she suggested.

Over dinner, Sarah began to realise the depth of Gowan's misery and began to sympathise with him. It was so easy to forget that he had a son who was 'missing presumed dead'. He was flesh and blood, and he suffered; he needed compassion and support.

They talked of the war, of the Military Services Act compelling married men to join the forces and of the Military Medal being awarded for bravery to those below commissioned rank. Sarah felt particularly sorry for him when he told her about his experience with the Whitby Tribunal. He had been told to appear before them to justify his employment of Anthony Harland. Gowan became animated and angry when he explained.

'Between us, young Anthony who's twenty-one, a boy o' nine years and me look after 200 acres including ninety-five arable. In other parts o' t' country, that'd be ample. But here it's different. T' land's unforgivin' and hard, and we all work more than most. I suppose I should be grateful they accepted my claim and let Anthony stay on, but they told him he had to join t' Volunteer Training Corps. Poor fella. By t' time he's done a day's work wi' me, he doesna' need to be paradin' around with a gun pretendin' to be a soldier. Anyways, at least I've kept him for now.'

Sarah listened to his outburst, watched his tired features and exhausted body. Suddenly, she made a decision. 'I tell you what we should do, dear,' she said. 'What would you say to Annie joining us at Flowergate? That would give my fragile daughter a chance to build up her strength. What do you think?'

Gowan looked at her with real gratitude. 'Tha'd do that for me?' He looked unsure of himself.

'No!' Sarah was quick to correct him. 'I would do that for you both, and particularly Fran. I worry about her. Don't forget that in Whitby I have my other daughters ,and they do more than their share of caring for these little ones.' She smiled. 'I believe they enjoy it!'

Annie was thrilled when she was told that she was going to return to Whitby with her grandmother. She would be joining her older sister.

When Sarah told Fran of the plan, Fran wept. 'Oh, Mother, thank you. But I feel such a failure. Look at Mary Pickering at Low Flask Farm. She will help me again when my time comes, but she has never had the sort of support that you and the rest of the family offer me. Oh, how I wish I was a stronger person.'

When Sarah returned to Whitby, she explained the demands that Thorney Brow put on Gowan and of his determination to keep the farm going. She said that she had to admire his strength of character and physical prowess but that they, as a family, should offer him and Fran the help they needed.

Lily promptly made a derogatory remark about Gowan, but Sarah defended him. Her daughter laughed. 'He's brainwashed you, Mother!' she exclaimed. 'You are such a snob! And you are so Victorian! To you, any untoward characteristics in a man can be forgiven if he has a healthy bank balance. The moment you heard that Gowan was becoming a wealthy man, your attitude towards him changed.'

Sarah wondered if there was any truth in Lily's accusation for she had to admit that she had been impressed when he had spoken of buying a villa in Robin Hood's Bay. But even Lily had to express her sympathy for Gowan when, in the middle of June, she heard of a new turn of events.

The postman brought a letter to Thorney Brow. It was an official communication and, without opening it, both Fran and Gowan were sure they knew the content. They were right: it was the confirmation they had expected but dreaded. It declared that Lance Corporal Gowan Pickering was dead.

They both knew they had been delusional, and recognised that the faint hope they had harboured was unlikely to become a reality. Yet when the news came, it was still a shock.

Sarah felt a fresh wave of sympathy for Gowan when the news, complete with a photograph of Gowan and a brief summary of his record, was printed in the *Whitby Gazette* under the headline, *Roll of Honour*. She carefully cut out the article and pasted it into her scrapbook.

Gowan insisted that his wife would rally as the summer sun warmed the land and brought a glow to her face. He made sure that she was relieved of work in the dairy and even took over the chickens. 'T' children'll be visitin' any time soon,' he would say.

The question of whether Herbert, Kathleen and Annie should visit the family was settled at the beginning of July, when Fran went into labour. Mary Pickering had agreed to help and was duly sent for, and on Friday, 7th July a girl was born.

Gowan resigned himself to the fact that he did not have a boy to name after himself and his now dead son and, as he had with Lilian's naming, he left the task to his wife. Fran decided to call the baby Mary.

Gowan was tolerant of his family's involvement with Whitby but made no secret of his opinion that it was a temporary arrangement for his children. One evening, he stood looking out across the bay. An owl hooted as the sun cast long evening shadows across the rough terrain, and a summer mist obscured the distant horizon. He could hear livestock shuffling into position for the night and tiny mammals rustling through the undergrowth. He puffed his pipe, leaned against a dry-stone wall that he had repaired that very day and felt content.

'What more could a human being ask for? This is where my children belong. This is where we turn our backs on the hubbub of the town and the lunacy of those who create conflict. I'm not going to be beholden to the Booths when I have a legacy like this to offer my children. T' folks of Whitby might as well enjoy them while they can, but they'll be home soon. Fran'll be fine. She just needs a bit o' rest after t' last confinement, and quality food – and that's something we can offer. There's nothing better than good, fat pork, and we're not short o' thick creamy milk neither.'

NINETEEN

AUGUST 1917 WAS an unseasonably poor month in Whitby. The war had all but destroyed the tourist trade, and the few hotels, landladies and sellers of souvenirs who defied the odds and tried to make a living all agreed that this weather was 'the final straw'.

In the parlour of 50 Flowergate on the evening of a wet and windy day, the family was sitting together after supper with their cups of tea reflecting on the day. Lily had been sewing. The Church Street Infant School where she had started teaching was on holiday, and she was enjoying the break.

Sarah looked at her daughter's handiwork. 'You must be psychic, dear!' she remarked. 'How did you know that you'd be needing your winter coat in the middle of August? I see you've turned that old coat of yours into a specimen of modern fashion. I like that. Muffs are so outdated, I believe.'

'Thank you, Mother. Yes, I've used the beaver fur from my old muff to trim the collar and cuffs, and I've altered my skirt too,' Lily announced proudly. 'I've decided to move with the times. Look.' Lily held her skirt against her body. 'The skirt is the new recommended six inches from the ground, and the hem measures two and a half yards round. What do you think?'

Sarah's smile evaporated. 'You mean you intend to wear it like that? I thought you were going to cut up the skirt to make something else.'

Lily laughed. 'Oh, Mother! Of course I intend to wear it like this. That's why I've gone to so much trouble to alter it. This war has taken over everyone's lives but I'm not going to let it take over mine. I want a bit of fun and a bit of glamour.'

Sarah was unimpressed. 'John,' she commanded, 'tell her. She might have a man friend who's encouraging her, and her new job might give her enough money to spend on fripperies, but she's still a Booth and Booths do not behave like this. It is just not appropriate for a girl to show her ankles!'

John peered over his newspaper and looked at Lily. 'The stitching on that hem is very professional, Lily. And you've done the fur on your collar and cuffs justice.'

Sarah sighed. She mused to herself, 'John is such a fine tailor and his only interest is in the quality of the work he sees before him. But he does tend to favour Lily, because she's our youngest, I suppose.'

At that moment, Rose arrived. She burst through the front door and, within minutes, was chastising Lily for spending time worrying about her appearance when there were people in dire need of help who possessed neither a coat nor a decent skirt. 'Anyway,' she declared, 'it's not that cold. It just feels cold in the wind. More worrying is the rain. Do you realise that, as we speak, our boys are in Flanders and the terrible weather means that they may well be suffering, just as they did when that beautiful poem was written about them?'

Lily immediately remembered the poem that Rose was referring to. She put down her work and recited the familiar words.

'In Flanders Field the poppies blow
Between the crosses row on row.'

'Oh, Lily! The words are so sad and so beautiful. They make me want to cry,' said Mary, remembering the first time she had heard the poem.

'How I wish this war would end. It seems there's no progress, no sign of a conclusion, and it makes me feel so helpless.' Lily's earlier look of pleasure disappeared as she considered the reality of war, but her face became quizzical as she asked, 'Do you think the Americans will make a difference now that they've joined us?'

'I can't believe the captains and generals would allow a repeat of that terrible time, Americans or no Americans!' Mary answered. 'Do you remember, we went to the cinema to see the film about the Battle of the Somme? There was a scene showing a dead officer whose dog stood over his body and refused to leave? It was so very moving. In that film, we witnessed for ourselves the bravery of the rank and file soldiers. They suffered such hardship, but they did it with such dignity. No – we should be so proud of them, and I'm sure their leaders have learned lessons from the past. That morass of mud in Flanders was a one-off.'

'Well, it's 1917, they're still in Flanders and the weather's terrible, so I wouldn't be too sure,' Rose chipped in. 'I agree with you though, Lily, I wish there was more talk of peace. It has to be said that Mr Asquith didn't seem to have a plan, and I was disappointed about that. But I'm not sure that Welshman, Lloyd George, is going to fare any better.'

'Well, if there were any sign of peace, we might be able to have as much sugar in our tea as we want,' Sarah commented. 'Though I doubt that shortages of sugar and, more recently, flour will lead to an amnesty! Which makes me think of poor Fran. How on earth do you think they're faring at Thorney Brow? Gowan might have done well out of wartime prices, but he'll not be best pleased with all this rain at harvest time.'

'Thank goodness Gowan agreed to Herbert, Kathleen and Annie going to school at Cliff Street. Them staying with us during term time must help Fran,' said Lily, her face creased with worry.

'A lot of farmers wouldn't have agreed to that!' Sarah remarked. 'They usually think an education makes children discontent.'

Mary gave a knowing smile. 'I think it was Fran's doing. You know she wants them to have a good start, and Father read in the paper that Howdale School is under investigation because of poor attendance and poor performance. Fran knows the struggles of the children at that school better than most. Those poor bairns had some terrible journeys to get there. At least her children won't have that problem.'

The Booths speculation was well placed. At Thorney Brow, Gowan was in the midst of bringing in the harvest during one of the wettest summers on record. On the evening that the Booths were discussing his fate, he arrived back to the farmhouse at the end of another wet day and flung his boots across the kitchen floor.

'This blasted weather's no good for t' crops, Fran. We're workin' flat out, we're doin' everything in our power, but it's hopeless. Rain, rain, rain! I canna' remember a worse summer. T' corn in t' stooks is rottin', and the uncut stuff's worse 'n useless. How's a man supposed to mek a livin' in these conditions? And on top o' that, there's not enough labour to deal wi' it all. Did tha' hear? T' Tribunal in Whitby's told my Reg's only hand to join t' Volunteer Training Corps. T' likes o' them haven't got a clue. My son's only helper'd be better usin' 'is gun t' kill t' vermin as teks our chickens.'

Fran hesitated. She was used to his moods, his exhaustion, frustration and anxiety, but she hated to see him tested to the limit. There was little she could do; after Mary's birth, she had been struggling to cope. Her desire to send her three oldest children to Whitby to stay with the Booths during term time had not been purely altruistic.

Now, she had another concern: she was pregnant again. Mary had been an easy baby to rear and Lilian, although still a frail little creature, seemed to have outgrown her early difficulties. But another baby would drain Fran's strength and she knew it. To cope with a two year old, a one year old and a newborn was a daunting prospect. Adding a dreadful summer to her problems was compounding them to an extent she could barely contemplate.

Gowan looked at her. 'What ails thee lass?' he asked.

'I think it is my pregnancy, Gowan. My back aches and I know my children are being neglected. I don't seem able to keep on top of everything. I thank God for Tamar. She was your youngest until you and I married, but she's been such an asset. She's left the Tyreman's and her home to come and help me nearly every day, and she's washed, cooked, cleaned. But I still feel inadequate and out of my depth. I feel such a failure.'

Gowan looked taken aback. 'Nonsense, lass. Tha's only doing what comes naturally. Tha'll be fine. Don't run off wi' t' idea that you're like my first wife, Tamar. She died in childbirth but she did na' have the help that you're getting from tha' folks in Whitby, and she did na' have a lovely home like Thorney Brow. You mark my words – all the signs are that tha'll finally give me a son.

'I need another son. I've thrashed young Herbert to within an inch o' his life for his attitude, but he's still a mystery to me. Only t'other day, I'd been tellin' 'im that chalk on t' fields helps t' turnips to swell, and he told me he didn't care!

'I reckon tha' folks in Whitby are part liable for his problems. Your Lily's teachin' 'im to play t' piano! What use is that? They've had too big an influence on him, but at least them lookin' after him saves thee some work. Cheer up, lass.

'Now then, I'll eat me dinner and be off t' Falcon. Tha'll have a nice quiet time on tha' own while I can grumble about t' weather and t' harvest and t' government wi'out bothering thee wi' my problems. And I keep tellin' thee to mek more use o' t' bairns. While they're here, Kathleen can tek care o' t' chucks, young Herbert can get hisself in t' sties to help wi' pigs, and they can still help thee. Bakin's not t' problem it is to townsfolks. Let Kathleen do as much as she can and Herbert can tend t' stove.'

Gowan chuckled. 'We might hope King George thrashes his cousin, but we canna' blame t' weather on t' war! And t' prices in t' shops ha' nearly doubled, so we're not doin' so badly as many!'

As he sat at the kitchen table and ate hungrily, Fran watched him. His complaints about the weather were real and his tiredness was real, but she knew that, regardless of his protests, he was enjoying himself. He loved nothing more than to pit himself against the elements and feel the power of his muscles as they wrenched a living from the land. He took pride in his independence and his mastery of his acres. To him, to be tested was a challenge.

Her own challenge was to survive the rigours of the life she had chosen. Her body had once been neat and trim, but five pregnancies had made their mark; now it felt too frail for the sixth baby she was carrying. She knew she looked older than her years, and she felt that her love of the moors had been a fantasy, an illusion. Reality was very different and she had been tested and found wanting because she lacked the instincts and experience of women brought up in a rural setting. She wondered if her marriage had been the result of an over-fertile imagination. In reality, her life had become a drudgery.

As Gowan left to saddle his horse and ride to the Falcon, she reminded herself that at least she could take pride in being the wife of a hugely popular, successful and respected man. Herbert joined her as soon as he knew his father had left.

'You should try harder to see the good in your father, Herbert. He works so hard, and is so proud of his farm and his family. He's a man to be reckoned with in these parts.'

'I don't care,' Herbert replied. 'The followers of the hunt who think so much of him don't get a thrashing like I do.'

As the summer came to an end and the autumn term began, Herbert, Kathleen and Annie returned to Whitby. Gowan took them to the station at Robin Hood's Bay and, despite her nagging doubts about allowing them to go, Fran admitted to herself that their departure was a blessing.

When Gowan returned, he brought with him a stoutly built, middle-aged woman carrying a suitcase. 'Now then, lass!' he called to her. 'I've brought thee a surprise.'

He beamed with pleasure, helped the lady down from the cart and introduced her. 'This is Miss Cooke, Fran. She's our new housekeeper. I'm not the insensitive man that tha' family thinks, you know! I've seen thee work and I've seen thee struggle. I think Miss Cooke'll be the makin' o' thee. Go and put t' kettle on, lass, and you two ladies can get to know each other over a brew.'

When news of the Pickerings' new housekeeper reached Whitby, it was the main topic of conversation. Lily was furious. 'Typical! He should have consulted Fran! Fancy having a total stranger appear and being told she's going to live with you and be your housekeeper! He's a bully!'

Sarah was more conciliatory.

'Gowan must be able to afford such a luxury. I think we should welcome any help poor Fran can get. That farmhouse is a nightmare and so remote. Last winter was dreadful, and it might be just as bad this year when Fran's giving birth.'

'Here we go again!' Rose was of Lily's mindset. 'The price of potatoes is a record high, flour is nearly impossible to come by, and whilst Thorney Brow might have plenty of eggs, nobody else can get hold of them. Farmers like Gowan are profiting. Just because he's got money, he can get away with anything in your eyes, Mother. Lily's right. He should have asked Fran's opinion.'

'But don't you realise, he's getting to be very well known across Fylingdales and even beyond? People respect him. The last time the Staintondale Hunt met, Fran told me that Gowan had a lovely brooch made for her out of the paw of a fox they'd killed that very day. He thinks a lot of her. And he's not only invested in that villa in Bay Town that he was speaking of – Fyling Villa – but he's rented it out to the doctor. Now the people of Fylingdales have a surgery, which they'd lost when old Dr Ross moved away. Perhaps we should be proud that he's a member of the family.'

'Well, I'll never respect him!' Lily was adamant.

Fran's initial reaction to the arrival of Miss Cooke had been panic, but that was a short-lived emotion. She soon discovered that the lady was built of solid, Yorkshire common sense and she was easy company.

Over a cup of tea, Miss Cooke weighed up her new employer and her new accommodation.

'You have a lot on your plate here, Mrs Pickering!' she remarked. 'This old place'll take a fair bit o' heating and a lot o' elbow grease. And I see you're not the sturdiest of critters yourself, if I might be so bold.'

Fran squirmed. She felt she was being judged. 'It was a harsh winter and a wet summer,' she defended herself. 'Gowan reckons both have been as bad as any he's ever witnessed. And I've never been one of those women who've had the good fortune to have muscular, strong bodies. I'm a town girl. I never grew up to understand country ways. Gowan used to call me his little schoolma'am!'

Fran laughed at the recollection and gave her companion a sideways glance. She did not want to appear rude by staring at Gowan's new employee, but she was conscious that, in theory, she should be asking the questions. The lady's clothing was of quality, her demeanour implied a practical appreciation of life, and she exuded self-confidence. Fran decided to take the initiative. 'May I ask you to tell me more about yourself?' she asked.

It appeared that Miss Cooke had a long history of service. Yorkshire bred, she had been housekeeper to a number of families in the county and Fran warmed to her as she spoke. 'Perhaps,' she thought, 'this is what I need. Some real, practical assistance.'

Within a short period of time, her thoughts proved correct. Miss Cooke had views on the role of a farmer's wife and articulated them, to Gowan's delight. She brought back efficient control of the dairy, kitchen garden and farmyard, and even suggested that Thorney Brow would be ideal for keeping bees. Apparently, she had experience in beekeeping and waxed lyrical on the advantages of having heather moors on the doorstep. Gowan assured her that he had considered it, but was of the opinion that he had enough to do without the added burdens.

Miss Cooke turned Herbert's bedroom into her sanctuary but declared that she would 'make alternative arrangements' if and when the necessity arose. Within days her presence was calmly and effectively turning Thorney Brow into an efficiently run farmhouse. She was a hard worker, a strong woman, and a huge asset.

She made soft mash for the chickens every morning, scattered grit, ensured they had fresh water and, to Lilian's amusement, as the days turned colder she hung a cabbage from the roof of their winter home in an outhouse to make them jump for exercise. She understood Gowan's anger when the blacksmith at Hawsker's military service exemption certificate was withdrawn when he had failed to attend the Voluntary Training Corps in Whitby.

She and Gowan were very much 'birds of a feather' and, for the first time since she had become mistress of Thorney Brow, Fran felt at ease with her home and the farming life it demanded. She had to admit that Miss Cooke's capable and experienced presence had removed the feelings of inadequacy and isolation she had suffered but denied. She was happy.

As autumn days saw the farming community of the moors recover from the traumas of the summer, there was a spirit of positivity in the taverns and farmsteads. To Gowan's delight, grouse shooting was good, meaning a fine return on the land he had rented out for shooting. He and Miss Cooke recollected the days of 1912, when twenty-five brace of foxes had been killed, and they decided that 1917 was not far off that number.

In October, the clocks were put back one hour to return them to Greenwich Mean Time. The previous year, a government initiative to save energy through what they had termed 'British Summer Time' had been introduced, and Gowan had been furious. He had insisted that animals do not respond to government initiatives and that the whole, ridiculous idea was simply an inconvenience to farmers who did not need an extra problem to deal with. Now, for the second year, Fran listened to his outbursts but, although she understood his frustration, she was hard-pressed to involve herself with his problems. She was feeling the effects of her pregnancy. She was tired and felt big and clumsy. She wanted the ordeal to be over.

'Oh that this earth with all its glory was less demanding of the humans who live amongst it,' she thought. 'Perhaps my baby will see a new world – one with less strife. Perhaps it will see advances in farming that will end the back-breaking work that poor Gowan and his kind have endured. This war cannot go on forever but surely it will ensure a sound financial future for us. I am lucky. I can see a good future for us all.

On 7th November, Fran gave birth to a boy. He was, of course, named Gowan.

TWENTY

AT THORNEY BROW the atmosphere was tense following baby Gowan's birth. Fran was ill. Sarah offered to keep the oldest children in Whitby when the school broke up for the for the Christmas holiday but Gowan refused. 'They'll do fine, woman!' he protested. 'It'll do em' good to pull their weight and, God knows, I need all t' help I can get.'

Miss Cooke did not complain but had an air of one who was containing her thoughts, planning a strategy. One evening, some days after Gowan's birth, she spoke. 'Sir!' she addressed Gowan. 'I need to speak my mind. Your wife is a sick woman. Little Gowan's birth has been a terrible ordeal for her. She has lost a lot of blood and she is weak. She has had enough pregnancies. Her body was never built for such. This must be her last. No more babies!'

Gowan had finished his meal and was intending to sit in peace and smoke his pipe. He looked less than pleased. 'I thought I knew thee better than this, lass!' he responded. 'I'll thank thee not to interfere with that which is none o' thy business. Tha's a good woman, and I'm beholden to thee for tha' work. Tha's been a blessing to this house, but I'll not ha' thee tellin' me how to run my life. Fran's a fine, intelligent woman. I'll agree she's not t' sturdiest, and she's not a country lass, but I give her all she needs in t' way o' good food and a good home. From now on tha'll keep tha' thoughts to tha' sen. And while tha' thinks on it, I'm off to t' Falcon. I'll not be told what to do in me' own house!' He put on his coat and boots, wrapped a

210

scarf round his head and left.

Miss Cooke heard him saddling his horse in the yard. She was not surprised at his reaction, but she was satisfied. She had meant what she said and was glad she'd plucked up the courage to say it. 'I'll not broach the subject again,' she decided. 'But what I said needed saying.'

In her bedroom, Fran lay with her newborn baby and listened. The thick walls of Thorney Brow muffled voices, and she was conscious that the children had been unusually quiet; nevertheless, she was sure she heard Gowan.

'That man's voice is so loud,' she thought. 'I hope he's in good humour, for I'm of little use and the winter weather is a hard taskmaster. Thank God Miss Cooke is here. I feel so weak, so helpless. Surely nothing ails me more than simply the business of giving birth. I know I've lost a lot of blood, but I believe a lot of women do so. I will recover, I know I will.'

The Booth family in Whitby were in disarray.

'Poor Fran,' Sarah looked distraught. 'There's nothing we can do. When I visited her, her tiny baby looked so fragile and she looked so ill, but Gowan was insistent that they'd cope. I just hope he's right.'

'Well at least Miss Cooke is there.' Like her mother, Lily was worried. 'I know I objected to the way Gowan introduced her to Fran, but I have to admit she's been an asset.'

'Rose says there are many women in Whitby who suffer even more than Fran,' Mary interjected. 'And they don't have a Miss Cooke to help.'

'We know that, Mary, and we know they often die giving birth. I just wish there was a way of stopping the constant cycle of childbirth that seems to be a woman's lot. I'd love to marry my Bert, but I don't want what Fran's got. I want a life of my own.' Lily looked disconsolate.

'Well, you should talk to Rose about that.' Mary looked puzzled. 'She says there are ways ... but I've no idea what they are!'

'That's enough, dear!' Sarah was visibly shocked. 'We don't talk about such things in this house, and Rose should know better.'

Lily said nothing but secretly decided to have a word with Rose on the subject.

'Rose, is it true that a woman can decide when to have children?' Lily asked her a few days later.

'I believe so,' Rose was quick to respond. 'But I'm not sure exactly how. I know a lot of women swear by breast feeding. They say it stops conception, but I'm not sure that works. There's another rumour that Beecham's Pills help, and there's a clever device called a diaphragm which is used with a sort of chemical called spermicide. They say that one of the doctors in Whitby sells the stuff to wealthy clients. Have you noticed that rich people seem to have smaller families than the poor? Perhaps this device works. But I know why you're asking – it's because of poor Fran, isn't it? You'd think Gowan would have enough money to let her see a doctor, but you know what he's like. He doesn't believe in doctors and I suppose he'd be afraid of the scandal if anyone found out. Anyway, he prides himself on being a virile countryman!'

'I don't want to be like her when I marry Bert. I don't want to have baby after baby, and I'm frightened of abortions. Is it true that you have to use a candle from the church to make abortion work?' Lily looked concerned. 'I play the organ in a church and I could easily get hold of one of the thin candles that I've heard are the right ones, but it sounds very frightening.'

'Why don't you just do what Fran seems incapable of doing, Lily? Just say no!' Rose chuckled. 'You're a lot stronger personality than Fran. She's always been such an airy-fairy sort of person. Do you remember when she first told us about Gowan. She rattled on about the beauty of the moors and landscape, and used to try to capture the scenery, wildlife, cottages and farms in her needlework. She said there could never be a more beautiful place on Earth. Mother used to be furious. She thought the moors were populated with people who were all heathens and uncivilised savages. Trust Fran to go and get herself pregnant! I tell you, Lily, she's never had much strength of will.'

Rose suddenly changed her tone. 'I tell you what, though, Lily, I wish I had her problem. You know George and I would love a family. I know Mother says I'd never cope – she seems to think a good mother has a tidier house than mine, and I know we haven't got any money. But we'd manage somehow.'

'Oh, Rose. I know you'd like a family, but I'm a bit like Mother. You and George can't even feed yourselves. And be honest, that house of yours is a disgrace. Why don't you clean it up a bit?'

'I didn't expect a lecture, Lily! You get in a clutter yourself with your sewing and handicrafts, and Mother's a fine one to talk. She's got books and magazines and stuff all over the place. But anyway, I don't have time. I've joined the League of Bread Savers, and I'm doing my bit for the Suffragettes by serving teas at their whist drives. Oh, and I'm supporting the Church of England Waifs and Strays Society by making sure those poor bairns get into the army. They deserve a future.'

'You're unbelievable, Rose!' Lily looked horrified. 'Surely you don't want to help young lads join the army! They'll get killed. This terrible war's not over yet.'

'They'll earn a good wage and they'll be housed and fed. Really, Lily! You know they'll probably die an early death anyway, so they might as well do their bit for King and country.'

'So long as you don't bring them back for Mother to feed!' Lily retorted. 'Which reminds me, have you bought food for yourself and George this week? Mother wasn't too pleased when you turned up again last Sunday lunchtime and said you hadn't got anything in the house to eat!'

213

◆ ◆ ◆

The winter of 1917 to 1918 was one of the severest in living memory. On the snow-clad moors of Fylingdales, sheep were lost, cultivation was impossible, and homes and outhouses became shelters for assorted animals. Miss Cooke ensured that the family housed lambs brought into the farmhouse for warmth, and she had no objection to Gowan's dogs joining them. She understood that farmers needed their dogs but couldn't house them in purpose-built kennels as many of the wealthy members of the Staintondale Hunt did. She further endeared herself to him by admiring his latest acquisition, a fine painting of one of his horses.

'You're quite the lord of the manor!' she remarked. 'That picture'll look good on the parlour wall. This place really is a credit to you and, with a bit of luck, this summer'll be an improvement on the last and we'll look forward to a good harvest. Life's not too bad, I reckon.'

Gowan beamed. 'Aye! Life on t' moors is not so bad is it, lass?' he agreed cheerfully.

As the green shoots of spring replaced the monotonous whiteness of snow, Fran was happy. Her home was now the welcoming place she had always wanted it to be and her children were thriving. In May, she even found time to visit places that she had held dear in years gone by. She climbed the steep slope to the moors one warm afternoon and delighted in the wild daffodils and bluebells that danced in the gentle breeze as she breathed in the clear, salty air. She watched curlew, golden plover and gannets and felt sad that Gowan set traps to destroy the raptors for, despite their glorious plumage and dramatic flight, they were responsible for killing grouse. A sea fret hovered over the cliffs and its cloud lent an air of mystery to the coastline. To her, this glorious place was as lovely as it had been when she first encountered it, and it renewed her energy and revitalised her feeling that this was where she wanted to be.

On one of her visits, Lily remarked on the changes she witnessed. 'You're looking so much better these days, Fran.'

'Oh, yes! I'm so happy, Lily,' Fran responded. 'I think a lot of it is because Miss Cooke is here for me. Tamar was a huge asset and she still visits, but she could only pop in when she had time. And she didn't make rabbit pies like Miss Cooke's! Gowan is so good with his gun and she makes full use of the results. You know, Lily, a lot of people think that Thorney Brow is isolated and that I never see anyone, but Gowan's children by his first wife call and update us on their progress, and Mary, his brother William's wife, has been a huge support. If you remember, she was with me at childbirth. When I had Gowan she was invaluable, for that was a difficult time.'

Lily returned to Whitby feeling as confident as she ever had that Fran's life was beginning to be the dream she knew her sister had always had. On her way home, she watched the light sparkle on the sea, the gulls circle overhead and the fresh, pale green shoots of the new season bring the promise of new life.

She heaved a sigh of relief. 'Please, God, let Fran's life be easier and more comfortable than I ever thought it could be. Let her enjoy the privileges of life with a man who might not be my choice but at least has the wherewithal to offer her and their children a fine future.'

In Whitby, talk was of the latest news of the war. The Germans had launched a major offensive in the hope of achieving a breakthrough before the Americans had time to organise themselves effectively. Casualty figures were high. The *Whitby Gazette* was a constant reminder that places previously unheard of were where local boys and men had met their end.

Sarah complained, 'Just as the weather turns fine, the fishermen bring in good catches and the farmers look forward to a decent harvest, we have to suffer yet more bad news. The market's still not what it used to be. There's a shortage of men to mend the roads and deal with the day-to-day running of many a business. On top of that, there are families left with no breadwinner, children with no father, and parents grieving the loss of their sons. We see too much of it here in the town. I don't want to see another memorial and I don't want to hear of another loss. Please, God let us have peace.'

◆ ◆ ◆

As spring ended, sheep were sheared and haymaking began at Thorney Brow. Gowan looked forward to the annual auctions where he hoped wartime prices would be reflected in a healthy profit. 'We're hogmen,' he reminded Fran one day when he came in from the yard. 'And my forbears were sons o' hogmen. I wonder if my little son will be a hogman. I declare it could be likely. I'll mek sure he's given t' right start.'

'Perhaps you'll have another to rear with that promise,' Fran remarked. She gave him a sideways look that implied that she had news for him. 'I'm pregnant, Gowan. Perhaps you'll have another boy by December.'

'Well I never!' Gowan looked pleased. 'Tha's a sight to behold, lass. We're a force to be reckoned wi' on t' moors, and I reckon I'm goin' t' be a legend in t' Pickering clan. Wi' Tamar's eight and your seven, I'll be t' father to fifteen bairns!'

Gowan paused then continued. 'Don't get me wrong, Fran. I'm minded o' t' responsibility. There's a lot o' mouths t' feed and tha's not t' strongest. But there's a summer t' look for'ad to and we'll mek sure tha' gets t' best, lass. Tha' can rely on me.'

Fran was less certain. She had delayed telling Gowan her news because she had hoped she was wrong, but she was not. The prospect of another confinement was daunting. She was

216

unsure if she should tell Miss Cooke. 'I'll tell her a bit later. She'll not guess just yet,' she decided.

As usual, August was a month Gowan relished, providing the weather was reasonably kind. Harvesting was back-breaking work, but compensation came on the 'Glorious Twelfth' when grouse shooting began and on other days when the hunt met. He loved it. He came home from the inns where the men met in the evenings with jokes and anecdotes, and was full of good humour even when the stories were about his own shortcomings.

He was particularly fond of one such story. 'They say I've got a loud voice,' he commented one evening. 'Tale goes that t' officers o' t' hunt got stuck in a bog. They yelled for help, but I'm told no-one went to their aid because they thought it were me calling t' me dogs! Can tha' believe it?'

He roared with laughter and Miss Cooke smiled. 'Well, I can't say I'd disagree, sir. I heard you calling for young Annie the other day and she covered her ears. But at least we can reckon your lungs are in good fettle, and there's no harm in that. I do believe Kathleen's going to be a chip off the old block. She can call in the cows, and the dogs obey because they hear her loud and clear. Having a voice like that'll stand her in good stead if she does what she says and stays on the land.'

Gowan smiled with pleasure. He turned to Fran. 'I wonder if our next little 'un will have a voice like that,' he remarked.

Miss Cooke looked stunned. 'No!' she said. 'Surely not!' She turned to Fran. 'Is it true?' she asked.

Fran nodded.

'Well, I wondered. You've been looking tired, your face looked thinner, and yet I thought you'd put on weight. I guessed you were nauseous a few weeks ago, but you hid it from me – or you thought you did. Oh dear, oh dear. How will you fare?'

'She'll be just fine and there's an end to it,' Gowan was quick to respond.

Miss Cooke looked unconvinced. She sat for a moment in silence and then burst forth with a tirade. 'I cannot stand aside and let this pass without comment,' she said. 'I said when little Gowan was born that there should be no more babies. This is too much. You, Mrs Pickering, can't stand another confinement. Why, oh why have you done this? And have you no thought for your other children? They need a mother who can care for them, they need her guidance and love. You can't offer this if you are unwell.

'I've given you all the support I'm capable of, and together we've transformed this house. Now there's a good chance you'll throw away all that effort because you'll be bed-bound again, and I'm not sure I want to be responsible for everything if you're indisposed. Am I supposed to look after baby Gowan? He's not a year old yet! Am I supposed to look after Lilian? I don't suppose you've noticed because you're too involved with the baby, but she's not walking well and she complains of pain in her legs. I'm sure she's got rickets. I didn't say anything because there's not much we can do about it if she has. Little Mary's only just had her second birthday. Oh, dear! This is too much.' Miss Cooke covered her face with her hands and her body swayed with emotion.

Both Gowan and Fran were taken aback. For a moment both were speechless. Gowan broke the silence. 'I told thee a long time ago, woman, not to interfere in my business. Now, you've disobeyed me, and I'll not have it. I'll not take criticism from anyone, and certainly not from the likes of you. You've been a damned fine housekeeper but tha's overstepped the mark. Tha' asked if tha' was supposed to be responsible for my home and my family while my wife gives birth. I'll tell thee now – no. Tha' can pack tha' bags and leave. We'll manage. Go, woman, go! Tomorrow'll do nicely!'

'But – but – I can't! Where will I go? How will poor Mrs Pickering cope without me? No! No!' Miss Cooke shook and then burst into tears. 'You're a cruel man. If you don't want me, you should look for someone else. Think on, sir. Think on!'

But Gowan was adamant. 'I'll tek thee to Bay Town tomorrow. I'll pay thee enough and there's an end to it.'

Miss Cooke fled to her room.

Fran was dumbfounded. 'Oh, Gowan, what shall we do? I've got so used to that woman. I think she's right, I don't think I can cope without her.' She wept, but she knew her husband. Once Gowan had made up his mind, he seldom changed it.

'Nonsense!' he declared. 'None of us is indispensable. We'll get young Tamar to help. She used to come here and tha' said tha' sen she was a real asset.'

As autumn brought its glory to the moors, sea shore and farmlands of Fylingdales, and as russets and browns replaced the greens of summer and swathes of purple heather, life at Thorney Brow became increasingly difficult. Fran was too fragile to appreciate the change of season and too involved in running the farmhouse to notice its beauty. Tamar did as her father asked and helped. The Booths cared for the three oldest children, which meant they barely saw their home, much to Kathleen's annoyance. As her time drew near, Fran knew that the ordeal she was about to face would be the biggest challenge of her life.

November saw a dramatic change in the war. On the 9th, Kaiser William of Germany abdicated, and the next day Kaiser Charles of Austria-Hungary followed suit. On the eleventh hour of the eleventh day of the eleventh month, the war was over. The population of Europe heaved a sigh of relief.

In Whitby, Sarah commented, 'Thank God it's over. I really don't care who's won.'

'Oh, Mother!' Lily looked horrified. 'All these years of hardship, of loss of life, and you don't care. You should be proud to be

British. We won!' She paused. 'But at a terrible price.'

On the moors of Fylingdales, Gowan greeted the future with mixed emotions. 'We've wasted enough life on this war. We farmers have been inundated with bits o' paper from t' idiots who like to tell us what t' do. Why, only recently there's bin a shortage o' feedstuffs for t' animals, and t' price o' wool's been down. Perhaps now they've got no excuse to interfere, we'll get back to doin' what we do best and just get on wi' it. But they'll never replace t' good 'uns who've been taken. I can't see farmin' ever bein' properly t' same again.'

At the end of November, Sarah made a decision. 'I'm going to move into Thorney Brow,' she announced. 'Fran will give birth soon. I know Mary Pickering has said she'll be there for her, but that poor girl needs all the help and support she can get.'

'But what will Gowan say?' Lily looked unsure. 'I doubt he'll welcome you with open arms, Mother!'

'Nonsense, dear! Whatever his reasons for getting rid of Miss Cooke, he knows help is needed. You and Mary can cope with the children and the lodgers, and even Rose might rise to the challenge if you need an extra pair of hands. I think it's my duty – and I've known Gowan long enough to deal with him.'

True to her word, she joined the family at Thorney Brow and Gowan accepted her presence. 'At least this new little Pickering will be born into a world of peace,' she remarked.

'Aye. I see a good future for 't lads. I allus worried lest more o' mine would be taken from me. I reckon we'll ha' a good Christmas this year, Sarah. They're already preparin' in Bay Town, and doubtless in Whitby too.'

'Yes. For the first time in years, we can genuinely hope for peace on Earth and a happy Christmas,' she agreed. 'In fact, I'll join you with a glass of something to celebrate, Gowan.'

◆ ◆ ◆

On Friday 6th December, 1918, the ordeal of childbirth began again for Fran. For the seventh time, Mary Pickering came to Thorney Brow to act as midwife. Sarah remained downstairs listening for every sound from the bedroom above. She fed Lilian, Mary and baby Gowan, and tried to ensure that their presence did not intrude on the events that were unfolding. Unusually, the children gave her no pleasure, she had lost her own appetite, and Mary seemed to need no support or help.

Outside, dull, grey skies seemed to complement her feeling of helplessness. In the kitchen, the tasks that she completed were meaningless. She thought she heard the sound of a baby's cry, then she thought she heard Mary speaking to Fran. Time seemed to drag; it was an interminable wait. She wondered why Mary had not called to her and told her how her daughter was faring.

At last an ashen-faced Mary came downstairs and joined Sarah in the kitchen. Her hands were shaking. She said nothing as she virtually collapsed into a chair near the fire and held her head in her hands. She ignored the little ones; Lilian, sensitive to atmosphere, shrank from her presence.

Sarah's instincts told her what had happened, though her whole being refused to accept what she knew. She looked at Mary's face, her look of defeat and quaveringly asked what she knew was a stupid question, 'How is she?'

There was silence. At last, with words that were barely audible, Sarah said, 'She's gone, hasn't she?'

Mary nodded. 'So much blood! So much blood!' she murmured. 'But the baby's alive.' She struggled back to her feet. 'Come. We need to care for it.'

Sarah's world disintegrated. Her beautiful daughter was dead. Her body suddenly felt weak and she shook as she helped Mary and did what was necessary. At first she did not weep but busied herself with the immediate problems of a newborn and the terrible sight of death. But then, she was angry, with Gowan, with Fran herself, with the injustice of it all. As the reality of the situation penetrated her confused mind, she wept in a way she had never wept before.

Neither the family in Whitby nor in Fylingdales had the Christmas or the future that they had anticipated so eagerly. The baby was named Francis in memory of his mother, and was given to Rose. Lily never forgave Gowan and accused him of murder, insisting bitterly that the baby should never have been conceived. They all looked to an uncertain future. Life at neither Thorney Brow nor Flowergate would ever be the same again.

EPILOGUE

I AM FRAN's granddaughter and, like my brother and cousins, was brought up on stories of Thorney Brow. My mother was Annie, or 'Nan' as she preferred to be called. She and her siblings, particularly the girls, had a close bond and boasted of their Yorkshire heritage and independence of spirit. Yet each, as they told and retold stories of their lives, repeated the same theme: they all agreed that they had been subjected to cruelty, deprivation and hardship.

At the time of their mother's death, Herbert was ten, Kathleen eight, Annie six, Lilian four, Mary two, Gowan one and, of course, there was baby Francis whose birth had led to Fran's death. The Booth family gave support immediately. Fran's sister, Rose, unable to have children of her own, was delighted to be given the newborn. Herbert, Kathleen and Annie, already enrolled at Cliff Street School in Whitby, were used to spending time in the town and continued to stay. But the youngest three were little more than babies and, within a matter of weeks, Gowan employed the first of what was to be a series of housekeepers to look after them.

Later in life Francis, or Frank as he was known, doubted whether being taken in by Rose had been a blessing. 'She was kind enough,' he would remark. 'But it's a wonder I survived. She wasn't what you would call a natural mother. Life was chaotic and we often had no food in the house.'

Lilian and Mary would retort, 'Well, our lives were no picnic. The housekeepers hated us, Father had no time for us, and we pretty well looked after ourselves. Mind, none of those ladies

223

stayed very long. We can't even remember their names. They all claimed that the work was too hard and Thorney Brow was too isolated.'

Herbert, Kathleen and Annie considered themselves to be the luckiest. Sarah and John Booth gave them a home. Whilst Kathleen preferred country life and wanted to go back to Thorney Brow, she admitted that she was well cared for. Annie harboured a dream that she would become a teacher like her mother and loved her time at Cliff Street School. Gowan insisted that Herbert helped on the farm and the boy unwillingly returned to Thorney Brow during particularly busy times of year such as harvesting or pig killing.

He passed the scholarship for Whitby Grammar School. 'We remember him hiding in the toilet by the side of the house and Father yelling at him to come out,' his sisters recalled. 'He was trying to do his homework!'

In June 1921, two and a half years after Fran's death, Gowan married Ethel Hornby. By this date, Herbert was twelve, Kathleen ten, Annie eight, Lilian six, Mary five, Gowan three, and Francis two. The day after the marriage was vivid in the memories of the children. Gowan had made sure that all of them, apart from Francis, were present. Herbert, Kathleen and Annie travelled from Whitby for the occasion. Armed with a riding crop to ensure that they behaved themselves properly, their father lined them up in the kitchen of Thorney Brow.

Once he had their full attention, he announced that he had married Miss Hornby, they were to call her Mother and, from that date onwards, the family would be reunited apart from Herbert and Annie who would still go to school in Whitby, and Francis who would stay with Rose.

'She looked so young and pretty, but not the sort of person we could view as a mother and certainly not a farmer's wife,' Kathleen commented.

'She reckoned she was on to a good thing,' Mary remarked. 'Father was well respected in the area and she obviously thought she would be lady of the manor. She soon found out, though! We had no intention of giving her an easy ride!'

'She'd never have coped anyhow,' the others pointed out. 'She was too inexperienced to take on Thorney Brow, let alone a brood of recalcitrant children.'

'She treated us like farm servants and we felt we were in the way – a nuisance,' Lilian argued. 'I know I hated her. She made Mary hold a bowl to catch the pig's blood at pig-killing time even though it made her cry and she couldn't cook. I'm sure that's why I got rickets.'

'But you couldn't walk after you fell from the rafters in the barn,' Nan chipped in.

'Well, nobody asked for any medical advice and you had real difficulty walking after that,' Mary added. 'But you were impossible to feed anyway!'

'We all knew she liked a drink!' Kathleen recalled. 'I know I'm not quite like the rest of you because I liked the farming life and Father bought me a pony. We called her Kitty, and I just wanted to be outside with her. But Father always had a bottle of gin in the house, and she took full advantage of that! Perhaps she couldn't cook because she was so drunk.'

The marriage between Gowan and Ethel did not last long. Gowan developed lung cancer, was ill for many months and died on 21st April, 1924. He was fifty-eight. His funeral left a powerful memory. The cortège consisted not only of the hearse and family mourners but so many horses, carts and foot followers that it stretched the mile distance from the farm to the main road. St Stephen's Church was packed.

Gowan had achieved his ambition and bought Thorney Brow, but now the house, most of its contents, the farm, the animals, equipment and his haulage business were sold at auction.

The one person who had always loved Thorney Brow and the glorious landscape in which it lay, was Gowan's mother, Jane. On 22nd January, 1924, at the age of ninety-two, she died at Glenean in Hawsker having learned of her favourite son's death sentence of cancer. She was not, therefore, witness to the decision to sell the place she loved best, or to argue the alternatives. The children had, at various times, cursed her unbending set of values and her determination to uphold traditions that were at odds with a changing world. They had been in awe of her apparent indestructibility, her physical strength, her remarkable memory and, latterly, her longevity. Her presence had given their lives a sense of stability and continuity; now, they felt her absence. They felt alone with their anger and their sense of having been wronged.

Gowan's wife, Ethel, moved to a three-bedroomed house at Saltwick on the outskirts of Whitby. She agreed with the Browns, the new owners of Thorney Brow, that Annie would remain at the house temporarily to be nanny to their three children. Young Gowan moved to Thorpe, where his half-sister Tamar took him in. But Ethel took Kathleen, Lilian and Mary with her. Tales of her inebriation, which left her incapable of caring for them, became legendary and created a lifetime of resentment at her neglect and even cruelty.

It was at this stage that Fran's sister, Lily, had an influence on the girls' futures. She had married her sailor beau, Herbert Watson, and they had left Whitby when he started work for the Elderdempster Line sailing the west coast of Africa out of Liverpool. The Booth family never forgave Gowan for Fran's death, but Lily was the fiercest critic and was vociferous in her condemnation of the man she viewed as nothing less than a murderer.

'He knew poor Fran would not survive another pregnancy,' she said. 'He had no respect for her, or for any other woman for that matter. He'd already killed his first wife, Tamar. You'd have thought that was enough of a lesson! But, oh no! He went on to murder my lovely, intelligent, sensitive sister.'

Lily offered a home to the girls, first Kathleen and Annie, and, later Lilian and Mary, as they reached school leaving age. She and Bert had a son, John, but, the girls were still made welcome in their three-bedroom semi-detached house at 32, Bathurst Road, Liverpool. They all agreed that she changed their lives in a way that had seemed impossible and it was from there that each of them moved on.

Kathleen, or Kay as she preferred, became a housekeeper to a family in Wiltshire and, from there, met and married a farmer. Annie, known as Nan, worked for the Yates family looking after their son, Ronnie, a deaf-mute little boy. She married and stayed in Liverpool. Lilian trained as a nurse, moved to Hull and was followed by Mary. Lily never married but Mary did.

The boys stayed in the Whitby area. Herbert graduated from Manchester University and emigrated to New Zealand, where he became head of the School for the Deaf in Sumner, Christchurch. Gowan moved to the tiny village of Waverton, near Wigton in Cumbria, and worked on a pig farm. Francis, or Frank, worked as an agricultural labourer and eventually became poultry manager at the Lincolnshire School of Agriculture.

The sale of Thorney Brow marked the end of an era. A Gowan Pickering had been born in the house in 1767 and a marriage between him and a spinster, Ann, from Robin Hood's Bay had been recorded in the big family bible. Records of other occupants were spoken of with pride. Now, it was lost to the Pickerings for ever. Memories were not of the grandeur of the land or the family's position in society; instead, stories of cruelty, deprivation, insecurity and loss were engraved on the hearts of Fran's children, who were the last to call it home.

The Pearson Sisters.
This was taken by Dent
Photographers of 9, St
Ann's Staith, Whitby
circa 1880.
Left to right are Emmy,
Sarah (became wife of John
Booth and mother to Fran
and her sisters) and Polly.

Sarah and John Booth's
five daughters: Annie,
Rose, Mary, Fran and Lily.

Three Pickering children: left to right,
Herbert, Annie (seated) and Kathleen.

Five Pickering children: left to right, Lilian, Herbert, Annie (centrally positioned) and Kathleen - seated and holding baby Mary.

Below: Six Pickering children: left to right, Herbert, Annie and Kathleen (back row) and Mary, Gowan and Lilian (front row). This was taken on one of the days of the auctioning of Thorney Brow in 1923 and was the last time the children would ever be together.

Gowan Hodgson Pickering at a meeting of the hunt
and taken on the sands of Robin Hood's Bay circa 1920.